The Treasured Mailbox

How to Use Authentic Correspondence with Children, K–6

Caroline T. Linse

bee line
BOOKS

Heinemann
Portsmouth, NH

Beeline Books

An imprint of Heinemann
A division of Reed Elsevier Inc.
361 Hanover Street
Portsmouth, NH 03801-3912
Offices and agents throughout the world

Acquisition Editor: Cheryl Kimball
Production Editor: Renée M. Nicholls
Cover and Interior Designer: Greta D. Sibley
Decorative Embellishments: Stephanie Peterson and Greta D. Sibley
Manufacturing Coordinator: Louise Richardson

Library of Congress Cataloging-in-Publication Data
Linse, Caroline T.
      The treasured mailbox : how to use authentic correspondence with
    children, K–6 / Caroline T. Linse.
          p.   cm.
       "Beeline books."
       Includes bibliographical references.
       ISBN 0-435-08139-X (alk. paper)
       1. English language--Composition and exercises--Study and teaching
    (Elementary)--United States.   2. Letter writing--Study and teaching
    (Elementary)--United States.   3. Education, Elementary--Activity
    programs--United States.   I. Title.
    LB1576.L5516   1997
    372.62'3--dc21   97-600
                                                                   CIP

Printed in the United States of America on acid-free paper
02 01 00 99 98 97 EB 1 2 3 4 5 6

In memory of Papa,
who taught me the value
of letters

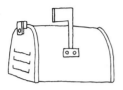

Contents

Preface ix

Acknowledgments xi

Chapter 1   *Welcome to the Treasured Mailbox* 1

Chapter 2   *A Class Correspondence Library* 11

Chapter 3   *Children's Books That Revolve Around Correspondence* 23

Chapter 4   *Pen-Friend Resources* 30

Chapter 5   *Resources for Free and Inexpensive Writing Paper* 37

Chapter 6   *Language Experience Approach to Correspondence* 42

Chapter 7   *The Architect's Perspective: Constructing Notes and Envelopes* . . .51

Chapter 8   *The Artist's Perspective: Creating Cards and Writing Paper* 73

Chapter 9   *Notes for Fun* 88

Chapter 10   *Cards That Double as Gifts* 105

References 129

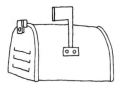

Preface

Dear Teachers, Parents, and Children,

I don't keep a journal, but I do write and receive correspondence every day. The pieces of correspondence that I send and receive chronicle achievements, crises, triumphs, and failures, reflecting a dynamic not found in many other types of writing. I also enjoy reading other people's letters, with my favorite collection being *Letters Home* by Sylvia Plath (1992).

I spend a great deal of my professional time overseas and rely on letters from friends and family for professional and personal sustenance. When I log onto the Internet and wait for the connection to be made, I often wonder if I am experiencing the same expectant feelings that pioneer women had when stagecoaches would roll in with the mail.

While the iron curtain was being swept away and the Baltic republics were reclaiming their independence in May 1992, I moved to Riga, Latvia. One day, as I walked toward my mailbox, hoping that there would be a letter from home, I saw flowers at the Freedom Monument in memory of loved ones who had been deported to Siberia. It was June 16. I ripped open Papa's letter and read about a baseball game and a recurrent rash that he compared to the results of picking poison ivy every day. As I walked home, I read and reread the letter until it was memorized. A few hours later, a call came. Papa's letter, tucked behind my passport, comforted me as I made the three-day sojourn home to his funeral.

I hope that this book will help your students or children make correspondence an important part of their lives.

Best wishes,

Caroline Linse

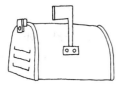

Acknowledgments

There are many children, teachers, and friends who helped with this project intentionally or inadvertently. I owe a great deal to children on several continents for field-testing the activities in this book. Professors and teachers from North America, Europe, and Asia lended their support. I am especially indebted to

Shirley Haley James, who provided unwavering support.

Katherine and Emily Ainsworth, who helped with research while I was off earning frequent-flier miles.

Barbara Barstow, who helped with the bibliography via the Internet.

Jane Knobel, who delayed lunches and dinners in order to discuss different facets of the project.

Wayne Linse, Elly Schottman, Fran Gamboa, Cheryl Katz, and Norma Overa, who put some of their own projects aside to help.

Janet, Jane, Silvija, Karen, Elliot, Ilona, and others, for providing letters for my mailbox and exotic morsels of food to keep me writing.

Marilyn and Berta, who helped when I wondered if there would be an end!

Michela, Christine, and Robert of Massachusetts.

Felix and Christine of Mexico City, and Leslie and Brianna of California, for providing correspondence.

Joel McKee, for taking photographs.

Julie, for remembering where the Federal Express office is.

My mother, who deserves a special thanks, for being a master teacher and writer in her own right.

CHAPTER 1

Welcome to the Treasured Mailbox

During the early 1980s I began teaching in rural Alaska, where I was introduced to the Alaskan version of the Bay Area Writing Project. Subsequently, writing was no longer a simple event with my students but a process that often began with me modeling writing. During personal writing time, I would sit in class and compose letters home to my family in California. My elementary ESL (English as a Second Language) students eagerly listened to excerpts from my letters. I also shared excerpts from letters from my parents. My students adored my father's irreverent gossip about neighbors and my mother's humorous poetry about everyday life.

These letters served as a springboard for intensive work with personal correspondence in class. I discovered that personal correspondence activities can be enticing and give children an opportunity to practice all steps of the writing process in real-life situations. My students experimented with different types of correspondence. One of the things that they discovered was that the painfully obligatory thank-you note or greeting card could easily be turned into an exciting project. My students also learned that there are many other opportunities to write authentic and meaningful letters. They were enthralled when they began to explore a variety of ways to "publish" their notes, cards, and letters. I was also pleased to find out that other teachers also view correspondence as an important part of a classroom writing program.

As a teacher and teacher educator, I have been collecting different ideas, resources, and techniques that will help children express instructions, information, feelings, histories, and questions through correspondence. And since correspondence isn't limited to words, children can explore a combination of visual and verbal methods of expression. As Donald Graves (1994) writes,

> In a corner of your life you maintain tools for your kind of expression. You savor your medium whether it is clay, wood, food, flowers, a well-exercised body, paint, cloth, paper or words in a play, and the smell is sweet. (4)

Whether you are a teacher, parent, or child, you should view this book as a guide to different tools of expression. The resources have been gathered from many corners of the globe and I have striven to make sure they are multicultural.

I certainly don't like to write all types of notes and letters. For example, there are times when I find writing a thank-you note to be an unwelcome chore. And students who are enthusiastic about other types of writing often groan when they have to write a thank-you note that is not heartfelt. What does a nine-year-old write to a relative who sent an expensive kindergartner's toy?

Unfortunately, this negative view of thank-you notes sometimes extends to all types of correspondence. This is in spite of the fact that some of the most meaningful information in our lives has been conveyed to us via mail. I have received job offers, school entrance notifications, letters of love, invitations to weddings, and even birth and death announcements by mail. Hopefully, this book will make the process of reading, writing, and publishing correspondence more enticing and rewarding for all of us.

This chapter includes some of my own thoughts about children, correspondence, and classrooms. I talk about some of the virtues of correspondence in the classroom as well as some of the nuts and bolts of implementing a writing program.

Chapters 2 and 3 provide children with models that they can refer to when they create their own notes, cards, and letters. Before children are asked to write and construct books, they spend a great deal of time reading books written by others. It is logical for children to also work with notes, cards, and letters prior to creating personal correspondence. Chapter 2 includes information on how to set up a correspondence library. Chapter 3 has an annotated list of children's books that revolve around correspondence.

Chapter 4 contains resources for both local and long-distance pen-friends. Suggestions for finding correspondents within your community are outlined. Also included are names and addresses of organizations that provide long-distance correspondents.

The aim of Chapter 5 is to help teachers, parents, and students locate free and inexpensive stationery, postcards, and greeting cards. Information on obtaining a wide variety of unused writing papers is included. Suggestions for recycling used greeting cards and postcards can also be found here. Chapter 6 focuses on different ways to publish language-experience stories (Dixon and Nessel 1983). Chapters 7, 8, 9, and 10 provide a variety of proven techniques that children can use to "finish" or publish their writing. Chapter 7 focuses on techniques that my students think are just plain fun, such as scratch-and-sniff cards. Chapter 8 describes some artistic ways of creating cards and writing papers. Chapter 9 looks at activities that require children to apply basic geometric principles. Finally, Chapter 10 consists of techniques used to make cards that can also double as gifts.

Real Reasons to Write

Correspondence gives children an opportunity to experience many different writing styles and purposes. I like to ask students why they think people write to or correspond with one another. Sometimes it takes a little prompting for them to consider the ways that correspondence is used, but eventually they come up with examples: the move of a friend can warrant a bon voyage card, or the birth of a baby may be heralded by a birth announcement.

Correspondence provides children with both a genuine purpose for writing and a specific audience. Children very quickly learn that the aim of a get-well card is to make someone feel better and that the audience is the ill person. They also discover a myriad of other purposes and audiences. (For a more comprehensive list of different types of correspondence see pages 12–16 in Chapter 2.)

There are a number of different children's books available that show children how correspondence can be purposeful and meaningful. *The Jolly Postman* by Janet and Allan Ahlberg and *Alfred's Alphabet* by Leslie Tryon use stories to illustrate the potential power of correspondence. (See Chapter 3 for a detailed list of children's books that revolve around correspondence.)

Writing and Relationships

Correspondence differs from many other types of writing in that it is ordinarily intended for a very specific individual or group of people, which gives children a personally meaningful audience. When children consider writing notes, cards, and letters, the potential audience for their writing expands to include family, friends, neighbors, and others. And these people are usually delighted with the correspondence they receive from children. In addition, children can develop new kinds of relationships, learn about the genre of correspondence, and even share other pieces of writing as they write letters.

In the following letter, Brianna, a fifth grader, transfers her pen-pal letter into a vehicle for thinking about writing and sharing her writing. She begins the letter by reacting to her correspondent's letters. She ends the letter by sharing samples of her own poems.

Brianna also explores the style of letter writing with this example. Her transitions are abrupt, which is more common and accepted in letters than in many other types of writing. She ends the letter with "Well got to go," the same way that many people move toward the end of a telephone conversation. This line would generally not work as well near the conclusion of a poem or short story.

Brianna is certainly using the letter to develop a personal relationship between herself and Ashley when she asks if she has told Ashley about what happened to her dog. This is also evident when she tells Ashley that she is going to bring something when the two girls meet.

4/26/96

Dear Ashley,

I liked your letters they were all great.

I don't know what I want to be when I grow up. But your plans that you [know] what to do when you grow up sound nice.

Yes, I think my teacher likes poetry a lot. But he did not teach us. A lady named Terri was teaching us. I did good in most of my poems. Also when I was home I made some poems in my room and I thought I would send you some. So I did. Hope you like them.

No body calls me four-eyes or anything else. Although my sister sometimes does when she is mad. But I don't mind that much.

I don't know if I told you or not that my family's dog died. Anyhow I just did. Well let me tell you about her. She was hit by a car. She was 2½ years old. She [was] part husky and German Shepherd. She was white and black. She was named Sheb. Anyhow we got a new dog. He is part Pointer and Australian Shepherd. He has a brown head and the beginning of his tail. The rest is brown and white spotted except a white [picture of a heart] on his forehead. (The brown and white looks like it is black and white.) His name is Rocky. He is fun to play with.

This summer we are going to go camping. We think we will go to Lake Tahoe. We will also go to my Uncle's wedding. The rest we are spending at home unless we are invited to something.

The 5th graders at the school are going to have an over night on June 5th. All the 5th graders are happy about it. My class is also going to go to the theater to see, "James and the Giant Peach." At school we are having our C.A.T. test. Which I don't like much.

Well got to go. 😦 Write again.

Sincerely,

Brianna

PS I will have something for you when my class meets your class.

Below are the writings enclosed with Brianna's letter:

Your good past

Don't count upon the frown to
let your good past go. But count
upon the smile to bring it back home.

In the spring

In the spring, I see
leaves growing on trees
and flowers blooming.

◉ PS: Write Back

Personal relationships with their audience can help children to become more involved and focused in the writing. The challenge is for the recipients of correspondence—the individuals who have a relationship with the child—to provide useful feedback to the writer. By having a relationship with the correspondent, the recipient is in a position to give both productive and heartfelt feedback, but most recipients do not supply much information. In my more frustrated moments, I have thought about enclosing a preprinted note with every piece of correspondence that my students create. The note might read,

> The words "I like it" do not suffice. Please give more of a response to the correspondent and the correspondence.

> Thank you.

Getting individuals to be more generous in their responses is a challenge. With some correspondence a written response is expected, as with sympathy cards. But with others, such as thank-you notes, a reply is less likely. In all cases, oral and written feedback assists writers tremendously, even if that feedback is indirect.

Fortunately, children sometimes ask for feedback directly. Parents and other family members can be nudged gently to respond to the children's correspondence. With a bit of encouragement, parents can give their own children very insightful feedback.

Writing and Other Forms of Expression

Greeting-card stores, museum shops, and art galleries sell beautiful cards designed to merge written images with visual ones. Such cards combine both oral and written forms of expression. Personally, I have found that beautiful notecards can be inspirations for writing. Many children respond in the same way.

An artistic child, writing a Mother's Day card, just couldn't get her thoughts together until she made a gorgeous bark-painting card. The process of making something attractive helped her to crystallize her loving feelings toward her mother. After the painting was finished, she wrote something that was especially meaningful to both mother and child. Connecting writing to graphic arts can raise both to new levels:

> Drawing and image making have been separate from the regular curriculum, treated more often as decoration than as tools for exploring the world and ourselves. But, when images and words work together to create meaning, literacy's potential expands. (Hubbard and Ernst 1996, 2).

There are countless ways that visual and verbal images can be blended together. Children enjoy exploring different ways to express themselves visually as much as they do verbally. Many children, even older ones, thrive when given opportunities to mix written expression with graphic techniques. I try to remind children to make the visual image and the words work together.

About the Activities

There are numerous types of activities included in Chapters 6 through 10. Basic instructions show how to do the activities. I also describe some appropriate occasions for different kinds of publishing and suggestions for children to incorporate various types of writing into the presentation. For example, if children are creating a pocket-style graduation card, they may want to add a homemade diploma. Many suggestions for multicultural correspondence are also featured.

Sharing the Techniques

Many techniques exist that children can use to share their thoughts through correspondence. There are three approaches that I use to share the strategies in this book with children. The first strategy is through workshops that teach small groups or entire classes several publishing techniques that the children can use to create their own correspondence. Often art teachers present the projects. The second strategy is to briefly demonstrate one or two activities to the entire class before children embark on a specific correspondence-writing activity. The third strategy is to put samples of different techniques in a correspondence writing center.

Computers and the Writing of Notes, Cards, and Letters

Until a few years ago, resumes and letters of application were always written out by hand in Britain. The penmanship of the applicant was considered part of the application process. In the United States, of course, typewritten resumes have been the norm for years. Almost all of the projects in this book can contain messages that were composed and printed on the computer, and notes and letters can be printed on the computer and then pasted into a card. Some writing paper can even be decorated by or before going through a computer printer.

Correspondence Writing Center

The lists that follow describe materials that can be included in a correspondence writing center. When I have had very small classrooms, I put writing paper in accordion files and other supplies in small, clear, stackable plastic bins. In large classrooms an entire corner of the classroom or an alcove can be devoted to a correspondence writing center. It is amazing how quickly a correspondence writing center can grow.

◉ Writing Papers

Children enjoy having different weights, colors, and textures of writing papers. Some fine stationery is very heavy. Another type is called *onionskin* because of its delicacy. There are also writing papers that have water marks that can be seen when the paper is held up to light.

There are many kinds of papers available in other countries that are not easily found in the United States—rice paper, luster paper (or paper luster), and two-sided origami paper. Nice paper can be a motivation in and of itself to go through all of the stages of the writing process.

◉ Envelopes

It is also very useful to have different sizes of envelopes on hand. There are legal-sized envelopes, letter-sized envelopes, A4 envelopes, greeting-card envelopes, and even miniature envelopes. Envelopes for hand-delivered messages can be any size. However, the U.S. Postal Service requires envelopes to meet minimum sizes for letters, and there are extra charges for letters and cards that are oversized. These regulations exist because the mail-processing equipment has limits. Notes, cards, and letters out of that range must be processed by hand.

◉ Stamps

A good collection of stamps is a must for any correspondence library, and a stamp collection can start with just one canceled postage stamp. In fact, canceled stamps are almost preferable for this purpose and make great models for homemade stamps on hand-delivered letters. Postage stamps reveal a lot about a culture and can even help children learn geography. International stamps are nice, but not absolutely necessary. However, if international stamps are included, you might display them on a world map with string that connects each stamp to its country of origin.

◉ Postage Chart, Zip-Code Chart, and Postage Scale

A postage chart listing the prices to mail letters, cards, and envelopes to different places adds credence to a correspondence writing center. Be sure to show postal regulations for minimum and maximum sizes for envelopes. A small food scale or postage scale can often be found for very little money at garage sales. Zip-code charts for local areas are often found in telephone directories. A chart listing zip codes of frequent correspondents can be made and displayed in the correspondence writing center.

◉ Writing Instruments

There are many different types of pens, pencils, and markers available. Children often enjoy finding the "right" one. Brushes are frequently used in Chinese, Korean, and Japanese writing.

CHAPTER 2

A Class Correspondence Library

I am delighted that the reading and writing connection is now being applauded in professional education circles. By reading literature, children develop an appreciation for stories as well as a sense of their structure. However, I feel that it is just as important to expose children to correspondence as to literature. Children frequently have an authentic need to write correspondence but are sometimes stymied as to how to do it. Often when we write cards and letters, the only models we have are those that have been written to us ages ago. When children read and have access to letters, cards, and notes on a regular basis, they begin to gain a sense of the genre of personal correspondence. In addition, it is also fun to read other people's mail. It is almost like eavesdropping on someone else's telephone conversation.

Taking a Field Trip to a Greeting-Card Store

One way of introducing the concept of a correspondence library is through a field trip to a greeting-card store. As an alternative, variety stores and pharmacies frequently have large

sections devoted to greeting cards and stationery. In any of these places, children can gain a sense of correspondence and look at methods of organizing the cards, gifts, and writing papers. Some children enjoy making a floor plan of the store arrangement to understand the layout more clearly.

Prior to the visit, ask the children to prepare a list of questions for the store clerks or managers. Who purchases greeting cards, stationery, invitations, and wrapping paper? What types of greeting cards are the most popular? This information may help children to think about the cards that they will create.

Soliciting Written Pieces of Correspondence

Setting up a correspondence library takes the same amount of time and patience as setting up a classroom library. Fortunately, the cost of setting up such a library is minimal unless a lot of fancy stationery and boutique-style greeting cards are purchased. The first step that I take when setting up a correspondence library is to solicit samples of correspondence from parents and other family members (Figure 2–1).

Once the personal correspondence starts coming in, children can place the items into different categories. When starting a correspondence library, it is sometimes easier to focus on one or two categories rather than many at once. Children may want to decide what types of correspondence should be included. Items that won't be included can be placed in storage. If at all possible, you may want to make a special effort to include correspondence that represents a number of exchanges. Listed below are some categories that can be used as individual sections for a correspondence library:

Appreciation Day Cards

Children's Day

Father's Day

Grandparent's Day

Dear Parents and Family Members:

Our class is in the process of putting together a correspondence library. The purpose of this library is to help children develop an appreciation for correspondence and also have models of notes, cards, and letters for the times when they must write their own.

We would appreciate it if you would send photocopies or original copies of all types of notes, cards, and letters. You may want to donate birthday cards, invitations, graduation cards, holiday cards, personal letters, postcards, or any other type of personal correspondence that you feel would be appropriate for children to read. Of course, only send cards, notes, and letters that are not too private. Private content can also be covered over with a black permanent marker or liquid correction fluid.

Only send originals that you were planning on throwing out anyway. Feel free to submit photocopies of other important personal correspondence.

We hope that you can visit our correspondence library when it is open.

Sincerely,

Mother's Day
Secretary's Day
Teacher's Day

Bon Voyage Cards
Congratulatory Cards
Anniversaries
Bar Mitzvah
Bat Mitzvah

> Birthdays
>
> Graduations
>
> New babies
>
> Retirements

Foreign Language Cards

Get-Well Cards

Holiday Cards

> Christmas
>
> Cinco de Mayo
>
> Earth Day
>
> Easter
>
> Halloween
>
> Hanukkah
>
> Kwanza
>
> May Day
>
> New Year's Day
>
> Passover
>
> St. Patrick's Day
>
> Thanksgiving
>
> Valentine's Day
>
> Yom Kippur

Invitations

> Anniversaries
>
> Graduations

Movies

Outings

Parties

Plays

Playdates

Trips

Weddings

Junk Mail with Appeal

Graphic-oriented mail

Personalized letters

Rebus words

Language-Experience Story Correspondence Cards

Birthday cards

Get-well cards

Thank-you notes

Letters to Advice Columnists

Letters to Children's Magazines

Letters of Recommendation

Letters of Request

Letters requesting assistance

Letters requesting information

Memos

Personal Notes and Letters

Letters between friends

Letters of introduction

Pen-friend notes and letters

Postcards

Sympathy and Condolence Cards

Thank-You Notes

Written Apologies

The issue of religious cards invariably comes up in public schools. In North America, I have preferred to have parents and students go through the cards and determine which ones they feel are appropriate. I see this as separating church and state and not as censorship.

I like including bilingual cards as part of a correspondence library. In many locations throughout the United States you can purchase greeting cards in languages such as Spanish, Russian, German, French, and/or Korean. Parents are often delighted to donate greeting cards in other languages.

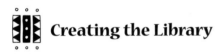 ## Creating the Library

There are a number of different ways that the correspondence can be compiled. Accordion files and shoe boxes work well. For me, the easiest way to store correspondence is in large manila envelopes attached to coat hangers. The coat hangers can be hung on hooks attached to a wall or to a closet door that is not opened very often (Figure 2–2).

 ## The Feel of a Library

There are a number of activities to help children view their correspondence files as a real library. The following pages discuss some of the activities that my students have enjoyed.

Figure 2–2

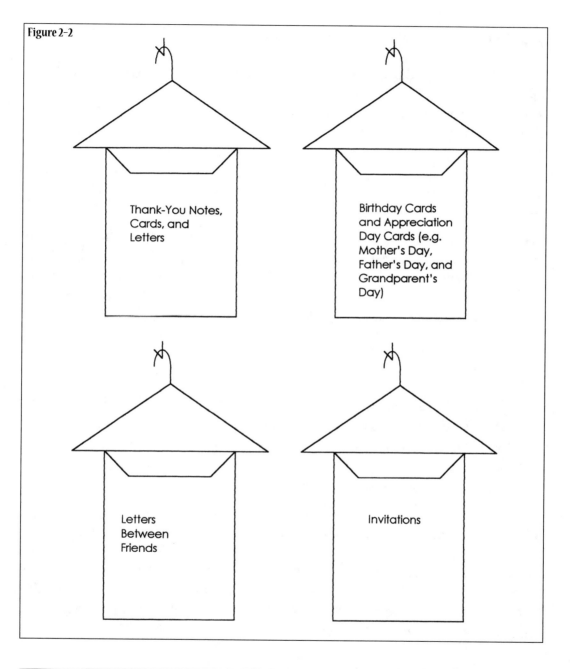

◉ A Classroom Event: The Correspondence Library Opening

Students may want to hold a Correspondence Library Opening Party. Children can send out invitations to all family members and others who have donated items. They may even want to make a plaque with the names of the founding members and/or contributors. Individual children or small groups of youngsters can prepare and conduct tours of the various materials in the library.

◉ Librarians

Many classrooms have a list of student helpers who take care of duties such as keeping the chalkboard clean, distributing lunch coupons, and taking notes that go to the office. Establishing an office of librarian who is responsible for the correspondence library may be a good addition. The librarian would put new pieces of correspondence in the library and keep it neat and reasonably orderly. Helpers could also take turns from week to week.

◉ Correspondence Library Guidebook

Children can make a guidebook for their library with a list of all of the types of cards included (see pages 12–16 for a comprehensive list of different types of cards). It can also have sample phrases from the correspondence and highlight favorite pieces of correspondence. The guidebook can be displayed in the library. There should be procedures for adding pages to the guidebook as new contributions are made to the library.

◉ Featured Pieces of Correspondence

Each month an individual child or a group of children may wish to select a greeting card, note, and/or letter to feature. These can be placed in plastic bags or behind an acrylic book holder (often sold in cooking stores). The children may want to write a list of criteria for their selection as well as a review of the correspondence.

Encouraging Reflection and Learning Through a Correspondence Library

Learning how to read and appreciate correspondence takes time and attention, which helps children to understand the genres as well as some of the subtle differences that often exist between spoken and written discourse. Children can work with correspondence and gain comprehension and critical thinking skills.

There are many different correspondence styles to master. One of the hardest things for me as well as for my students is deciding when to use the word *love* when signing off. On a larger sphere, it is necessary to consider the voice and format of each genre. Some correspondence resembles a story, unlike brief pieces such as thank-you notes.

Listed below are some questions that can be asked when children work with items from their correspondence library.

- What type of correspondence is this?

- How does the letter begin?

- How are people addressed (Ms., Miss, Mrs., Mr., Dr., or a first name)?

- What is the relationship between the author and the recipient?

- What is the purpose of the correspondence (to congratulate, to celebrate, to thank)?

- Is it a humorous or serious piece of correspondence?

- How long is the message?

- What, if any, transitions are used from paragraph to paragraph?

- What types of personal messages do people write on preprinted cards?

- Are there other types of writing, such as poems or riddles, included with the correspondence?

- How is the message signed?

- If there is a corresponding envelope, how is it addressed and to whom is it addressed?

▦ Correspondence Library Activities

Developing correspondence library activities will help children become more familiar and comfortable with the pieces collected in the library.

◉ The Correspondence of the Day or the Week

Just as there is time set aside for reading fiction in most classrooms, you might plan a time each day or week to read favorite pieces of correspondence.

◉ Awards for Different Cards

Your children may wish to create different awards for cards, notes, and letters or to have awards for the overall success of humorous, poetic, serious, and emotional messages. They also may want to evaluate the artwork and the overall design.

◉ Portraits of Recipients

Have children look at one or more pieces of correspondence directed to a specific recipient. Have children create a portrait of the recipient. Birthday cards work very well for creating portraits of individuals.

◉ Biographies of Recipients

Older children may want to look at one letter or several pieces of correspondence addressed to the same individual. Have children look at samples and then write a biography describing the recipient. In the biography, children might want to include the recipient's name, age, hobbies, and place of residence.

◉ Biographies of Authors

Ask the children to examine several different pieces of correspondence written by the same author; they do not have to be written to the same recipient. Then have them create a biography of the author. Later, children may want to evaluate their biography to see if it was accurate.

◉ Thank-You Note Analysis

Give each child a copy of a thank-you note written by a child or an adult. Have children draw a picture of the gift that the thank-you note was written about. Some children may also want to draw a picture of the recipient using the gift. Older children can write an advertisement for the gift.

Bilingual Cards

I like to ask children who do not speak the language of a specific card to try to figure out the meaning of its words by looking at the pictures. Have the children use removable labels to write what they believe the card says.

Children can also be encouraged to look at the different cultural writing styles often seen in cards in different languages. In Korea, for example, it is more common for acquaintances to greet one another with surnames instead of first names. In some cultures, individuals rarely write messages on commercially produced cards.

◎ Venn Diagrams of Different Greeting Cards

Children may want to compare two different cards using a Venn diagram (Figure 2–3). Two birthday cards work well.

Figure 2–3

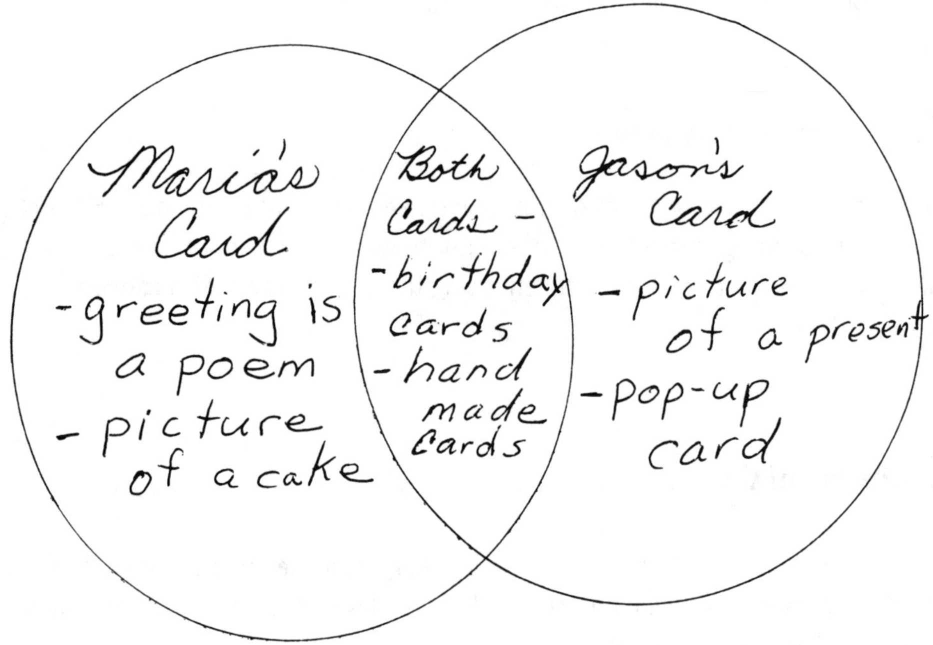

Maria's Card
- greeting is a poem
- picture of a cake

Both Cards -
- birthday cards
- hand made cards

Jason's Card
- picture of a present
- pop-up card

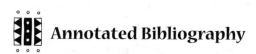

Children's Books That Revolve Around Correspondence

CHAPTER

3

There are many children's books available that feature correspondence. The following recommended books can help children discover the genres of personal letters, thank-you notes, letters of invitation, business letters, friendly letters, and get-well notes, to name a few. The books discussed in this chapter should be available through most bookstores in English-speaking countries. Any and all make a good addition to a classroom library, classroom correspondence center, or a school library.

Annotated Bibliography

Children's Picture Books with Correspondence Themes

Of the children's picture books that revolve around letters, several contain the actual texts of letters. Some books contain one letter; others have a number of letters exchanged. Blending letter writing with children's literature is an educationally powerful combination.

Ada, Alma Flor. 1994. *Dear Peter Rabbit.* New York: Simon and Schuster. Ages 5–8. This book consists entirely of very detailed letters among storybook characters getting ready for a birthday party for Goldilocks. The letters show how news can be shared, plans made, and concerns voiced through correspondence.

Argent, Kerry. 1991. *Thank You, Santa.* New York: Scholastic. Ages 5–8. This wonderfully illustrated storybook consists entirely of letters between Santa and Samantha, a young girl, over a one-year period. The book begins in January with a thank-you note written by Samantha to Santa. Santa responds with delight, and a year-long correspondence friendship between the two begins.

Caseley, Judith. 1991. *Dear Annie.* New York: William Morrow. Ages 5–10. This book primarily consists of a correspondence between a grandfather and his granddaughter. The book begins with a lovely card and note that Annie's grandfather sends to her right after she is born; other beautiful notecards are also included. The art and message are more powerful together than either alone.

Hample, Stuart, and Eric Marshall, eds. 1991. *Children's Letters to God: The New Collection.* New York: Workman Publishing. Ages 8–adult. This book is a collection of authentic letters children have written to God. The letters do not focus on any one denomination or religion. They are charming and very honest and illustrate how children can center their thoughts through letters. Due to the religious nature of this book, it may not be appropriate for all classrooms.

Henkes, Kevin. 1995. *Good-bye, Curtis.* New York: Greenwillow Books. Ages 3–8. This is one of my personal favorites. This story describes the last day of work and retirement party of Curtis the mail carrier. There is a very clever and surprising ending.

James, Simon. 1991. *Dear Mr. Blueberry.* New York: Macmillan. Ages 4–7. This charming book is about Emily, a young girl who goes on vacation and needs information about whales. She decides to write to her teacher for help and knowledge; a very convincing correspondence dialogue ensues. There is just as much tension in the correspondence as there is in any face-to-face dialogue.

Nichol, Barbara. 1993. *Beethoven Lives Upstairs.* New York: Orchard Books. Ages 5–8. This book consists entirely of fictional letters written by a young boy to his uncle from 1822 to 1824. The boy writes about a lodger—none other than Ludwig van Beethoven—whom his mother has taken in. The boy is both embarrassed by and intrigued with his upstairs neighbor. This book combines music, history, and art.

Rodell, Susanna. 1995. *Dear Fred*. New York: Ticknor & Fields. Ages 5–8. This story follows a letter from Grace, who lives in America, to her half-brother Fred, who lives in Australia. This book delicately talks about being separated from loved ones. The letter allows the reader to eavesdrop on the thoughts and feelings that Grace shares with Fred.

Schindel, John. 1995. *Dear Daddy*. Morton Grove, IL: Albert Whitman. Ages 5–8. This charmingly illustrated book is about a little boy named Jesse who lives across the country from his father. Jesse feels that telephone calls "go too fast" and turns to letter writing. He uses an old typewriter to craft a letter to his father. After what feels like a long wait, Jesse is delighted when he receives a letter from his father. The letter is so long it comes in a tube and is really a vertical mural.

Spurr, Elizabeth. 1996. *The Long, Long Letter*. New York: Hyperion Books. Ages 4–8. This is a beautifully illustrated and charming story about two sisters who live apart. One of the sisters decides to write a very long letter to the other sister, and the humorous tale traces its creation and delivery.

Tryon, Leslie. 1994. *Albert's Alphabet*. New York: Macmillan. Ages 3–7. This book clearly shows the power of a piece of correspondence. Albert is a school carpenter who is instructed to build an alphabet on the school playground. His instructions are given in the form of a memo from the school principal.

◉ Books with Removable Letters

There are a number of books available for children that contain envelopes pasted directly into the book with removable letters inside. These kinds of books are incredibly popular among children and inspire many to craft their own versions. Even reluctant readers adore pulling the letters out of the pockets and reading them or listening to them being read aloud.

They have several downfalls, however. Complicated production procedures make them expensive. Also, due to the heavy stock and thick envelopes, the book spines of many such books do not hold up very well. You may need to reinforce the spines with cloth tape or library tape. Children may easily lose or misplace the letters. I find that keeping the books in resealable plastic bags helps prevent the letters from becoming separated from the books. Numbering the individual letters and envelopes can encourage readers to correctly reinsert the letters into the envelopes. I also like to have children figure out how much each letter costs, which helps them become more responsible.

Ahlberg, Janet and Allan Ahlberg. 1986. *The Jolly Postman or Other People's Letters.* Boston: Little, Brown. Ages 4–adult. This is the first book in the Jolly Postman series and my favorite. It contains letters, postcards, and greeting cards written by different storybook characters. The text of the book is written in rhyme. This book eloquently shows how rhyme and correspondence can be combined.

Ahlberg, Janet and Allan Ahlberg. 1991. *The Jolly Christmas Postman.* Boston: Little, Brown. Ages 4–adult. This intriguing book includes Christmas cards, gift cards, and little presents in envelope pouches inserted directly into the book's binding. This book features pieces of Christmas-time correspondence among different storybook characters. One of the cards is a game board! The most imaginative piece of correspondence is between the Jolly Postman and Santa and Mrs. Santa, illustrating the Jolly Postman's journey.

Ahlberg, Janet and Allan Ahlberg. 1995. *The Jolly Pocket Postman.* Boston: Little, Brown. Ages 4–adult. This charming book contains special items from the Jolly Postman's mailbag. There are items for Alice in Wonderland, Dorothy from Oz, and other favorite storybook characters. This book shows students how a variety of different items can be included with correspondence.

Cartlidge, Michelle. 1993. *Mouse Letters.* New York: Penguin Books. Ages 4–9. This little book contains miniature letters written by mouse fairies. Children adore the smallness of the letters and handwriting. Each letter describes fairy life and contains clues to help the reader figure out where the next letter will be hidden.

Langen, Annette, and Constanza Droop. 1994. *Letters from Felix: A Little Rabbit on a World Tour.* New York: Abbeville Press. Ages 6–10. Felix, a stuffed toy rabbit inadvertently gets separated from his owner, a little girl named Sophie. Felix winds up taking a world tour of exciting and interesting places. Felix writes letters to Sophie about his adventures. This book is especially appropriate if children are studying or are interested in global geography.

Langen, Annette, and Constanza Droop. 1995. *Felix Travels Back in Time.* New York: Abbeville Press. Ages 6–10. Felix, a stuffed toy rabbit, gets lost at a museum in this story. His owner, Sophie, is very distraught because she has owned Felix for what seems to be "forever." Felix travels through time and all over the world and sends letters to Sophie describing his adventures.

Martin, Ann M. 1993. *Chain Letter.* The Baby-sitters Club Series. New York: Scholastic. Ages 10–14. This book clearly illustrates how notes, cards, and letters can be a valuable part of friendships. While the members of the Baby-sitters Club are away for the summer, they must figure out a way to communicate with one another. Their answer to this problem is a chain letter among the members of the club. The book consists of cards, notes, memos, letters, and even a friendship bracelet.

Potter, Beatrix. 1995. *Dear Peter Rabbit: A Story with Real Miniature Letters.* London: F. Warne and Company. Ages 5–adult. This delightful book tells the story of the lives of the characters in Beatrix Potter's books. As a way of delighting her young friends, Potter made up notes and letters among her characters. Text on the bound pages and letters inserted into envelopes convey the story. One of my favorites is Peter's letter to Mr. McGregor asking when his cabbages will be ready. Peter Rabbit writes charming letters but, like the other characters, doesn't follow the conventions of spelling.

Tolkien, J. R. R. 1995. *Letters from Father Christmas.* Boston: Houghton Mifflin. Ages 7–adult. This charming book includes letters that Tolkien wrote to his children at Christmas time. The letters are reproductions of the originals and are placed in envelopes. Each copy has the original text in Tolkien's hand on one side and a typewritten copy of the text on the other. The letters tell of events at the North Pole. Text on accompanying pages provides context. Drama, intrigue, and humor are contained in almost every letter.

◉ Chapter Books Based on Letters

There are some very good chapter books based on letters or the process of letter writing. These books help older children learn that letters can be used as devices to tell a story. The genre of letters is often more intimate than other types of writing. In the right context, letters can give authors a chance to be more direct and open about their thoughts and feelings.

Bat-Ami, Miriam. *Dear Elijah*. 1995. New York: Farrar, Straus, and Giroux. Ages 8–12. This touching story is told entirely through letters. Rebecca is a young girl who writes to Elijah about her father's hospitalization in the intensive care unit. Rebecca reflects on her father, her religious beliefs, her classmates, and even her own writing. Although much of this letter has the feel of a journal, the letter format helps to provide a focal point for the story.

Bunin, Sherry. 1995. *Dear Great American Writers School*. New York: Houghton Mifflin. Ages 10–14. This bittersweet story chronicles the development of a young woman who has enrolled in a correspondence writing course during World War II. Through letters to the Great American Writers School, Bobby Lee develops her own writing skills. In the end, it is Bobby Lee's own perseverance and tenacity—and not the writing school—that lead to her success as a writer.

Hesse, Karen. 1993. *Letters from Rifka*. New York: Puffin Books. Ages 8–12. This winner of the National Jewish Book Award tells the story of Rifka, a young girl whose family is forced to flee Russia in 1919 because of the brutal treatment Jews receive there. Through letters to Tovah, her cousin in Russia, Rifka tells of her traumatic and heart-warming journey to the United States.

Lyons, Mary E. 1992. *Letters from a Slave Girl: The Story of Harriet Jacobs*. New York: Simon & Schuster. Ages 8–13. This book shows how letters can be used to convey a vital historical perspective. This is a powerful work based on the true story of Harriet Jacobs, a slave girl who had her autobiography published in Boston in 1861. Author Mary E. Lyons retells Jacobs' story through letters spanning from 1821 to 1842. In letters written to her family, Jacobs, describes her courageous journey and escape from slavery as well as how she starts a new life.

Martin, Ann M. 1992. *Karen's Pen Pal.* The Baby-sitters Club Little Sister's Series. New York: Scholastic Books. Ages 7–10. This book is in the popular Baby-sitters Little Sister series and chronicles a pen-friend relationship between Karen and Maxie, who has a tendency to brag. Karen starts to make up things, which results in "real trouble." This book shows how the dynamics of a pen-friend relationship can be similar to the dynamics of a face-to-face relationship.

Van Leeuwen, Jean. 1989. *Dear Mom, You're Ruining My Life.* New York: Penguin Books. Ages 10–14. This novel is about the tribulations a young girl faces because of her "eccentric" family and her search to communicate through letters. Letters sprinkled sparingly throughout the story make the tension within key relationships seem more alive and real.

◎ Books Related to Correspondence

Levine, Michael. 1994. *The Kid's Address Book.* New York: Berkeley Publishing Group. Ages 6–18. This book provides children with the addresses of popular celebrities and interesting clubs, businesses, museums, magazines, and comic book publishers. This book also contains the addresses of organizations that assist kids with problems and the addresses of heads of state all over the world. This book is a must for a correspondence writing center.

Moss, Marissa. 1995. *Amelia's Notebook.* Berkeley, CA: Tricycle Press. Ages 10–13. This imaginative book is a child's journal, notebook, and scrapbook all rolled into one. There are a number of postcards and letters included in the scrapbook. These pieces of correspondence show readers how actual postcards and letters can be incorporated into a personal memoir.

Pen-Friend Resources

CHAPTER 4

Children adore receiving letters from pen-friends. I have seen even the toughest middle school boy melt upon receipt of a reply from his pen-friend. Pen-friends for children can be found in a classroom across town, at a local nursing home, or across an ocean.

Just as face-to-face relationships take time to evolve, so do pen-friend relationships. When people meet they usually go through a routine of introductions, and it takes time to figure out if they will be acquaintances or friends. This process also occurs when children are developing a relationship with a pen-friend. The nervousness of writing to a stranger resembles the fear of meeting someone new. Children need to carefully consider what part of themselves they want to share with their pen-friends, and they may want to create a semantic map such as the one shown in Figure 4–1 before they write their first letter.

Keeping a pen-friend relationship alive requires the same amount of effort as keeping up with an exercise program, diet, or music lessons. Even though I find letter writing to be a personal priority, I have been known to postpone having my students write back to their pen-friends when our classroom schedule becomes overloaded or frantic. It is helpful to schedule letter writing into the classroom calendar.

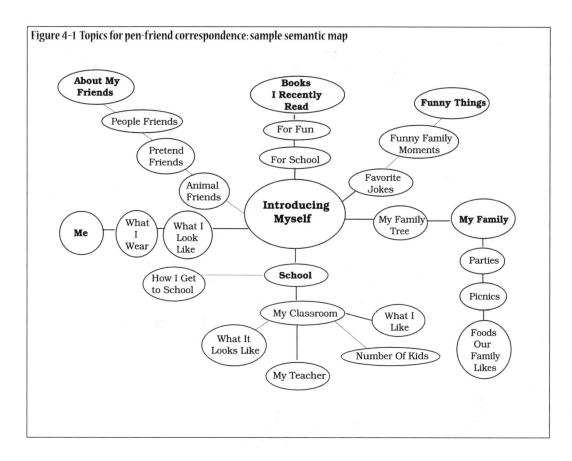

Figure 4-1 Topics for pen-friend correspondence: sample semantic map

Finding Local Pen-Friends

The following list contains some potential sources for finding pen-friends in your neighborhood, community, or county. One of the advantages of having local pen-friends is that it can be possible to build in a meeting at the end of a specific number of letter exchanges or at the end of a specific period or length of time. Children can meet their correspondents for an outing such as a picnic or a joint field trip.

Police officers can be pen-friends to individual children, small groups of children, or entire classes. Police officers are especially willing to be pen-friends in towns and cities with community- or neighborhood-outreach programs. Children often establish a big-brother/big-sister relationship with their pen-friend officer. The officer in charge of outreach programs can help match up children with potential correspondents. Unfortunately, not all police departments have time to participate in pen-friend programs.

Children who spend a great deal of time in and out of hospitals can form pen-friend relationships with healthy children. Individual children, small groups of children, or an entire class can be matched up with a chronically ill child. It can be problematic to match up healthy children with children who are terminally ill; many young children do not always have the emotional resilience to cope with a terminally ill pen-friend. The head nurse or head social worker of the pediatric ward of a local hospital are potential contacts for pen-friends.

Retirement home residents often enjoy being pen-friends to younger children. One child called them "grandparents by mail." Retirement-home residents generally have a much better sense of the genre of letter writing than younger individuals. Nursing-home patients can also be pen-friends, though some may not be healthy enough to participate in a correspondence relationship. The activity or social directors of local retirement and nursing homes can be contacted to find out if some of the residents would be interested.

Senior citizens who attend activities at senior citizen centers are often interested in being pen-friends. Hooking up with seniors through such a center can lead to an entire group of seniors corresponding with an entire group of children. The directors of local senior citizen centers may be able to set up a pen-friend project.

College students majoring in education can be pen-friends for elementary school students, and education professors sometimes require their students to form pen-friend relationships. The education students benefit by having an opportunity to establish a writing relationship with children, and the children benefit by having an adult to write to. The relationship can be very structured with an agenda aimed at helping the education students. Professors at a local college of education are a good source. It can help if college students are given an assignment to be a pen-friend for a specific period of time, or they may not be as likely to fulfill their commitment. You may also find that college and university students studying to work in the helping professions may be interested.

Shut-ins are individuals who do not leave their homes generally because of physical problems. Rabbis, priests, or other clergy can often give names and addresses of shut-ins who would make good pen-friends.

Companion classes can be set up with children at a different grade level in schools nearby or far away. Children in special education or bilingual classes or high school students can be pen-friends to elementary school students. An exciting variation is to match up with classes that are studying similar topics to your students. Teachers with your targeted populations can assist in setting up a companion class project.

Finding Long-Distance Pen-Friends

When using organizations to locate pen-friends, it can be unwise for children to give out a personal address. You may need permission from the principal for children to receive pen-friend correspondence at school .

All of the addresses below have been researched and, as of the copyright date of this book, are accurate. It should be noted that there are other organizations that match individuals, but many are not suitable for children and/or for classroom use.

World Pen Pals

World Pen Pals is a letter-writing service operated by the International Institute of Minnesota, a nonprofit organization. World Pen Pals matches students from the United States with more than 20,000, 12- to 20-year-old students from 175 countries and territories. As of this writing, the rate for one pen-friend was less than five dollars.

World Pen Pals
International Institute of Minnesota
1994 Como Avenue
Saint Paul, MN 55108

In addition to the fee, applicants must include a self-addressed legal envelope measuring nine inches by four inches. World Pen Pals does not give any refunds.

Preference is given to children who are able to write in another language. World Pen Pals does ask children to indicate a country of preference and their sex. Because children from every country are not always available, World Pen Pals cannot guarantee a pen-friend from a specific country.

Once children have submitted their applications, they will receive a name and address of a pen-friend, suggestions for letter writing, and the *Pen Pal Post* newsletter.

◎ Student Letter Exchange

There are two different branches of the Student Letter Exchange: one located in Minnesota and the other in New York City. The branch in Minnesota helps bridge cultural understanding by matching adults from around the world. This is a good resource for parental involvement. Many parents and other family members enjoy having their own pen-friends.

Just for Adults

Please note that the Student Letter Exchange branch in Minnesota is intended for adults desiring a pen-friend. They send out a directory of three hundred names of pen-friends ages twenty to fifty-four and a second directory of names of pen friends ages fifty-five to ninety. The directories are updated frequently and cost $8.95 plus $1.00 for shipping and handling. A self-addressed stamped envelope should accompany the order. Be sure to specify on your letter which directory you want.

Just for Adults
Student Letter Exchange
215 Fifth Avenue SE
Waseca MN 56093

For Children

This Student Letter Exchange matches students ages nine to twenty with children in other countries as well as the United States. Children ages nine and ten are generally only eligible for matches in the United States and other English-speaking countries. Students ages eleven to twenty are placed with countries all over the globe. One pen-friend currently costs $5.00.

A stamped and self-addressed envelope should be included with the request.

> For Children
> Student Letter Exchange
> 630 Third Avenue
> New York, NY 10017

Peace Corps Volunteers

World Wise Schools is a Peace Corps program that gives American students the chance to experience the world through the eyes of past and present Peace Corps volunteers. Students in grades three through twelve are matched with a Peace Corps volunteer in one of the ninety-four countries the Peace Corps serves. By corresponding with their volunteer, the teacher and class learn firsthand about another culture. The following letter is from a student to her Peace Corps correspondent:

Dear Kelly,

I like the slides. The slide that I liked best was the abalone shell. Some of the slides made me sad and some of the slides made me want to go to Gautemala. I liked the postcards. They are very cool.

School is a lot of fun and it is cool too. I learn a lot.

Do you like Guatemala a lot?

What is your favorite animal?

Well, bye.
Your Friend,
Leslie

Every year, more than sixty thousand students in all fifty states are involved. Since its inception, an estimated three hundred thousand students have benefited from the program.

World Wise Schools Program
1990 K Street, NW
Suite 9500
Washington, DC 20526

◎ Armed Forces Letter-Writing Programs

During times of real or potential conflict, the U.S. armed forces operate a pen-friend program between service members and civilians in the United States. During the Gulf War and the more recent Joint Endeavor (in the region of what was once Yugoslavia), school children from all over the United States sent messages to service members involved in these dangerous assignments. With Operation Joint Endeavor, individuals have been writing to service members and their families. For more information regarding any current letter-writing program operated by the U.S. armed forces, contact the office of your local congressional representative or senator. Similar programs have been offered in other countries with troops serving abroad.

◎ Science by Mail

Science by Mail was developed in 1988 by the Museum of Science in Boston, Massachusetts. This innovative educational program helps children around the world get hands-on exposure to a variety of science topics. The program teams children in grades four through nine with scientists who volunteer as pen-friend mentors.

The program is currently offered through ten chapters in the United States. However, anyone can join, regardless of where they live.

Science by Mail
Museum of Science
Science Park
Boston, MA 02114-1099

Sources for Free and Inexpensive Writing Paper and Cards

CHAPTER

5

My students and I like locating free and inexpensive (unused) writing papers, and we have found many sources. They also have fun collecting used greeting cards, notecards, postcards and labels that can be recycled. They view the search as a giant and purposeful scavenger hunt. This chapter's suggestions are based on what productive strategies we've found for locating unused paper and for recycling old cards and labels.

Recycling Used Greeting Cards and Postcards

Recycling Used Greeting Cards to Make Postcards

Pictures from many holiday and birthday cards can be reused. The greeting cards can easily be turned into postcards by cutting off the message printed or written inside the card. If the cardstock is heavy enough and not embossed, the picture portion can be cut off and instantly turned into a new postcard. If the picture portion of the card is embossed or on flimsy paper,

or if a message is written on the back of the picture, then the picture can be pasted on cardstock to create a new greeting card.

◉ Recycling Used Picture Postcards

Used picture postcards can be pasted on heavy construction paper or cardstock. Children sometimes like to write the preprinted information from the postcard on the back.

◉ Sources for Used Postcards and Greeting Cards

Retirement homes, nursing homes, and hospitals are often willing to collect greeting cards. Individuals may wish to cut off the message or note portion of greeting cards before donating them.

It is nice to have cards that represent different cultural groups. Some of my students, after the winter holidays, have brought unused cards and stationery back from other countries. Students who stay home during the holidays may ask family members or friends who will be visiting from other countries to bring them unused stationery and cards. Foreign-language cards can be used as a resource for producing a single bilingual greeting card or an entire student-made line of bilingual cards.

Sources for Unused Greeting Cards, Postcards, Stationery, and Writing Papers

◉ Garage and Tag Sales

Postcards, greeting cards, note cards, stationery, and envelopes can often be purchased at neighborhood sales. In many cases these cards are sold in bundles without envelopes. If the top and the bottom cards are a bit crumpled, check the ones in between. Children can make their own envelopes by following the instructions on pages 68–69 of Chapter 7.

⊙ Business Sales

Many companies that are going out of business have leftover letterhead. Similarly, companies frequently have to throw out their stationery if they have moved and their address has changed. Labels can be pasted over the company's name and address, or the company name on the top can simply be cut off. Companies are usually delighted to give stationery away if they know their name will not show.

⊙ Resume Paper

Many adults often have old resumes that are outdated and invalid. The old resumes can be used as liners for many of the projects presented in this book. Many adults also frequently have extra blank sheets of resume paper.

⊙ Hotels and Motels

Many different hotels and motels give away stationery as a way of advertising. The stationery is usually left in a folio or folder in guest rooms. Housekeeping staff and managers are often willing to give up a few dozen pieces of hotel stationery to teachers.

Parents and friends who frequently travel are also happy to collect stationery from hotels and donate it to a school or classroom. Letterhead from abroad is especially popular. It is fun to see how the name of a different country is written in the language of the country. For example, the Spanish word for *Spain* is *España.*

Children can also write letters requesting stationery from hotels in different places. Hotels can be contacted in a target city in the United States or overseas. To find the addresses of different hotels, call the 800 or 888 numbers of hotel chains and then write directly to the manager.

⊙ Trains, Airplanes, and Cruise Ships

Trains, airplanes, and cruise ships frequently have complimentary postcards and letterhead available. Sometimes their stationery shows vintage vehicles. Passengers in sleeping compartments are often provided with several sheets of letterhead with matching envelopes and several postcards.

⊙ Print Shops

Print shops often have bits and pieces of leftover papers and are often willing to give away scraps of different colors, textures, and weights of papers and cardstock. I personally like cardstock because the colors and textures are frequently more appealing than construction paper.

Many school districts have their own print shops, which are very willing to donate scrap paper for writing and art projects. The best commercial print shops to approach are those that work with high-volume jobs such as directories, catalogs, and corporate stationery. On occasion, print shops may donate envelopes with blemishes.

⊙ Wedding Shops and Stationery Stores

Many wedding shops and stationery stores have books of sample wedding invitations and other stationery. These shops and stores are often willing to give away the sample books when new ones arrive.

⊙ Chambers of Commerce

If children are studying about a specific city or town, they may want to request postcards and notecards that picture the region. Chambers of commerce in the target town are good places to start. Directory assistance can supply the telephone numbers.

Sources for Free Pictures for Greeting Cards, Notecards, and Postcards

There are many different sources for small and attractive pictures to make your own stationery. Children who believe in their heart of hearts that they cannot draw or do not have time to draw appreciative using pictures created by others.

◉ Regional Advertising Calendars

Many small calendars given by banks, restaurants, realtors, and chambers of commerce have beautiful pictures of nearby attractions. Some greeting card manufacturers also produce calendars. The pictures from these calendars can be cut out and mounted on art paper or cardstock to decorate greeting cards and postcards.

◉ Vegetable and Flower Seed Packages

In recent years commercial greeting-card manufacturers have designed notecards with seed package designs on the front. The picture of the flower or vegetable or the entire front panel or packet can be cut out and attached to note paper or cardstock to make attractive stationery.

◉ Perfume and Cologne Packages

Many of the labels on perfume and cologne bottles have pictures of pretty flowers or exotic-looking animals that can also decorate stationery and greeting cards. These labels can easily be removed by placing the bottle in a steamy bathroom. With extreme caution, a teacher, parent, or other adult can use a tea kettle to remove the label. Children may want to use the last drops of perfume or cologne from the bottle to scent any stationery they create with the label.

◉ Herbal Tea Boxes

Many herbal teas are marketed in beautifully illustrated boxes. These boxes often have pictures of flowers and plants as well as interesting names such as "Sleepy Time" and "Red Zinger." Children may want to cut off the pictures from the tea boxes and any tea bag inserts for decoration. They may also wish to incorporate the names of the teas into their message.

Language Experience Approach to Correspondence

CHAPTER 6

Children who are just learning to write can compose thank-you notes, get-well cards, and other pieces of correspondence by applying the basic premises of the language-experience approach (Dixon and Nessel 1983) as described here. Children who have no literacy skills dictate stories to a teacher, teacher's assistant, or parent volunteer. After the story has been written, children make pictures to illustrate the story. Some very young children can take the process one step further and compose their own authentic messages using invented spelling. Children delight in reading their language-experience stories over and over again. An example of one language-experience story, written by a student named Christine, is shown in Figure 6–1.

There are a number of occasions when it is especially appropriate for children to create language-experience story correspondence. After a field trip or a visit from a resource person, children can write a language-experience thank-you note. When a classmate has been ill, I like to have classmates create a language-experience story for her or him. Some classes like to adopt a senior citizen as the class grandparent or a student in another country as a class pen-friend. In both of these instances, children can make and send language-experience story correspondence. The following is an example of a class-authored language-experience thank-you note:

Christine

Wen I get Sike my Daddy
when I get sick my daddy

teYKS me to the toktr. We LdK too Poly tostthg.
takes me to the doctor. we like to play together.

We LaiK to WoCh tv.
we like to watch t.v.

Figure 6-1

Yesterday, we walked to the fire station.
We had fun.
I liked the cookies a lot.
Fire fighter Ramirez is a good cookie maker.
Fire fighter O'Malley showed us where he sleeps.
Fire fighter Jones came down the pole.
He was in a hurry.
The firefighters are nice.
Thank you.

Yours Truly,

Mrs. Green's Kindergarten Class

There are a number of interesting ways to publish language-experience story correspondence. Some techniques, such as the accordion-book language-experience correspondence story, are very simple and require no advanced planning, whereas a photo album language-experience story correspondence may require more preparation. The publishing suggestions in this chapter include

- Accordion-book language-experience story correspondence
- Story correspondence and audiotapes
- Language-experience story correspondence with tools
- Photo album language-experience story correspondence
- Cartoon language-experience story correspondence
- Language-experience story correspondence shape book

Special Notes About Language-Experience Story Correspondence

Envelopes for Language-Experience Correspondence Stories

When children begin to make language-experience story correspondence, they need to think about what size envelope they will use to send the correspondence. A very large envelope for the correspondence can be made by taping two poster-sized pieces of paper together.

Classroom Copies of Language-Experience Story Correspondence

It can be helpful to make copies of some of the language-experience story correspondence to be kept in a classroom library. Children can reread their own correspondence as well as that written by other children. These stories are especially useful to show to a parent volunteer or other adult who will be helping children create language-experience story correspondence.

Accordion-Book Language-Experience Story Correspondence

Frequently, language-experience story correspondence is displayed at the recipient's workplace or home. It is not uncommon to go into the office of a zoo and see language-experience stories hanging on the walls. Accordion-book language-experience correspondence works very well for this purpose because the entire book can be displayed on a wall or door.

Materials

Ruled paper, photocopier paper, or construction paper

Crayons, markers, and pens

Masking tape or cloth tape

Procedures

This type of correspondence needs to be written and illustrated on a number of different sheets of paper. After the illustrations and the writings have been completed, the book is assembled. When making accordion books it is especially important to consider the order of the pages because all of the pages will be viewed at the same time. Some children like to lay out all of the pages on a table or the floor. This way they can check and experiment with pages arranged in different orders.

The pages of the accordion book can be put together from left to right or from top to bottom. Children may want to think about where the language-experience story correspondence could possibly be displayed. If the book is going to be displayed on a door, then it is logical to bind them together from top to bottom. If the book is going to be displayed across a wall, then the pages should be put together horizontally.

The pages of the book can be laid out on a floor or extra-long table before they are bound together with tape. Once the pages are bound, the correspondence is ready to be sent or delivered.

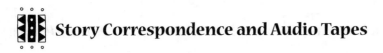 **Story Correspondence and Audio Tapes**

Children enjoy making audio tapes to accompany language-experience story correspondence such as get-well messages, pen-friend letters, and thank-you notes. Create the written correspondence first and then make an audio tape to accompany it. A pocket or envelope for the audio tape can be attached directly to the correspondence, and then both are slipped into the envelope. As a variation, children may want to make a video recording of themselves reading the story aloud.

◉ Materials

Manuscript writing paper

Crayons, markers, and pencils

Audiocassette recorder

Audiocassettes

Construction paper or lightweight cardstock for the book cover

Materials for making a sleeve or pocket to hold the audiocassette, such as heavy-weight legal-sized envelopes or special audiocassette mailers

A bell or other noise-making device to indicate when the pages should be turned

◉ Procedures

Have children create language-experience story correspondence. The entire story can be dictated to the teacher as the class listens, or the story can be written by having individual children dictate portions of the story to an adult. I always need to write down who said what or I forget, making it more difficult to arrange the audio taping.

After the language-experience story correspondence has been written and illustrated, the children are ready to make an audio tape to accompany it. Have individual children read each part of the story into a tape recorder. An adult should help with the recording process to ensure as clear an audio tape as possible. If the story is written on several pages, children may want to make a noise using a bell or another object to indicate when pages should be turned by the reader.

Once the story has been recorded, a sleeve or pocket is made to hold the audio tape. A legal-sized envelope can be closed and sealed, and then the end of one side of the envelope can be cut off to create a pocket for the audio tape.

Language-Experience Story Correspondence with Tools

Language-experience story correspondence is appropriate for thank-you notes for resource people who have come to the classroom or whom the children have visited. The correspondence is enhanced with hand-drawn pictures of different people and the tools they use. Models of those tools can be attached to the correspondence with short pieces of string.

Materials

Construction paper

Markers, crayons, and colored pencils

Scissors

Tape

Optional: Thread or string

Procedures

Have children create language-experience story correspondence about the resource person. Encourage children to brainstorm the different items or tools that the resource people use as part of their job, such as a bread pan for a baker. These items can be listed or drawn on chart paper as a semantic, word, or picture map.

Once the language-experience correspondence story has been created, have the children illustrate the different pages with pictures of the resource people. On a separate sheet of paper, children can draw tools for each of the resource people. These drawings can be attached to the pictures with small pieces of string and tape. It is helpful for children to label the different tools because the recipients may have trouble figuring out what specific tools the individual drawings represent.

Photo Album Language-Experience Story Correspondence

This type of language-experience story correspondence is especially appropriate for field trip thank-you notes. This correspondence consists of photographs taken during the field trip with text authored by children.

Materials

Camera and film

Crayons, markers, pens, and pencils

Construction paper or lightweight cardstock

Materials to mount photographs (picture-mounting corners or double-sided tape)

Optional: Materials for making an album cover

Procedures

Plan by having the children take photographs during the field trip. Once the photographs are developed, let the children decide which photographs they will use for their correspondence. A complete story can be written and illustrated with the photographs and hand-drawn pictures. Children may want to put their correspondence together to look like a photo album, complete with an album cover.

Cartoon Language-Experience Story Correspondence

Cartoon bubbles are a very simple flourish that children may want to add to language-experience stories. These language-experience stories include pictures of the recipients and the children (the authors of the correspondence). Speech bubbles are drawn above each person.

Materials

Construction or photocopier paper

Markers, crayons, and colored pencils

Optional: Removable sticky labels

Procedures

Have the children—either individually or in small groups—draw pictures of the recipients and themselves. Remember that the more drawings of people that are included, the more opportunities that exist for writing different speech bubbles.

If children are creating thank-you notes for a resource person, they may want to include pictures of things that relate directly to the person they are writing to. They should think about what the resource person talked about. For instance, if they are thanking a doctor and especially enjoyed listening to a heart, they may want to include a picture of a stethoscope in the picture. By including a picture of an item that relates to the recipient, it will generally be easier for children to remember what the recipient said.

When children have finished drawing their pictures, they are ready to fill in the speech bubbles. I prefer removable labels for the bubbles because children can make several drafts.

Language-Experience Story Correspondence Shape Book

Shape books relate the whole text to some theme of the language-experience story. A thank-you note to a painter who visited a classroom may have each page shaped like a palette, for instance.

Materials

> Scissors
>
> Tracing patterns
>
> Crayons, markers, and pencils
>
> Items for binding books together (e.g., cloth tape, string, yarn, drinking straws)

Procedures

Before children begin dictating or writing their correspondence, they should decide what shape would be the most appropriate for the message. For example, if they are sending a note to a tortilla factory, they may want to make writing and drawing paper in the shape of a tortilla. Often, I find that the shape being used is contingent upon what shapes that I or most students are able to draw.

Create (or have a child with artistic ability create) a pattern or template in the desired shape for the writing paper. Then cut out the necessary number of sheets with the template. Have children dictate the story as you write it down on the shape paper, or they can copy the story and print it directly. Part of the language-experience story correspondence can be about how the class decided what shape to use.

Children can illustrate individual sentences or parts of the story, or individuals or small groups can add illustrations following the text. All writing and illustrations should be put on the shaped paper.

Finally, children need to consider how their shape book correspondence will be bound together. If at all possible, include a binding that relates to the basic shape object. For example, if the paper is shaped like a glass of milk, drinking straws would be a fun way to bind the book together.

The Architect's Perspective

CHAPTER 7

Constructing Notes and Envelopes

Many commercially available greeting cards seem to be based on architectural principles with three-dimensional, pop-up, and movable-parts cards. Adaptations of these types of cards can be done in the classroom, and my more mathematically and architecturally inclined students adore them.

The activities in this chapter help children learn how to integrate different processes with pieces of correspondence, and many of the projects require a great deal of forethought, planning, and drafting. Some students will see these activities as a jumping-off point for constructing elaborate, even mystifying cards.

All of the cards and envelopes in this chapter demand more attention to measuring and to following a specific set of instructions than the projects in other chapters. But, by creating these cards and envelopes, children will have an opportunity to internalize different measuring and geometric concepts. These activities can be done in tandem with math units related to geometry and measuring. I personally like children to learn how to "guesstimate" measurements, using fingers to approximate sizes.

The projects increase in difficulty through this charter and include:

- Slip-ups
- Secret message notes
- Pop-up cards
- Pocket notes
- Mobile cards
- Pocketbook cards
- Flying object cards
- Designing envelopes
- Embedded envelopes
- Lace cards

 ## Slip-ups

An adult education ESL teacher from Santa Cruz, California, introduced me to slip-ups a number of years ago. They generally consist of one moving part that moves up and down to reveal different words to complete a sentence. The basic message can be contained in a single sentence with one variable word. This type of card is very easy to make and works well with beginning writers. It is also a nice transition for learners who have spent a great deal of time with predictable books and authoring their own versions of predictable stories.

Many beginning writers rely too heavily on the word *and* to link thoughts and ideas: " I like you because you are nice and kind and sweet and good." Slip-ups help children convey the same content without having to repeat the sentence pattern or stringing of words together. Children can write a basic sentence with different words that can be substituted in one part of the sentence. For example, a child may write,

	spinach.
	spaghetti.
I love you more than	pizza.
	strawberries.
	ice cream.

In this example, one incomplete sentence was written on the actual card and the words were ordered according to preference (Figure 7–1). When each sentence is read with words starting from the top to the bottom, the message becomes stronger.

Figure 7-1 Note that placement of the slip-up could be reversed so that one word at a time appears over the slots with remaining words hidden behind the card.

⊙ Materials

Construction paper or lightweight cardstock

Scissors

Markers, crayons, pens, and pencils

⊙ Procedures

Children need to plan the message, sentence or phrase that they will include in the card. Children can then draft one basic sentence and substitute one word in each line, considering the order of the words that will be included in the card. The food words in the previous example show how words can be listed according to preference. As a child pointed out to me, unless you are Popeye, loving someone more than spinach is probably not as meaningful as loving someone more than ice cream!

After children have drafted their sentence and the substitution words, they should plan the overall design of the card. It is important to consider whether the slip-up will be made on the cover of the card or on the inside message portion of the card.

To construct the slip-up, children draw two small parallel slits with enough space between both slits to see the word. Next children make the actual slip-up. I tell students that they may want to draw a dog's bone and then write their words on the main part of the bone. A bone shape works very well because the flared ends will not accidentally slip through. After children have made the bone and the slits, they are ready to insert the bone into the card.

This activity is especially appropriate for very young learners. It helps children internalize the concept of parts of speech. The activity can also be varied to meet the needs of children at the initial stages of writing. If children don't feel comfortable using invented spelling, they can copy down the base sentence and make pictures instead of words for the movable strip of paper.

Secret Message Notes

Secret messages can be worked into the overall design of a card in many different ways. Secret compartments should be large enough to accommodate a note but small enough so that they aren't too easy to find. A secret compartment can be as simple as an object with a back flap or can be as complicated as a secret or false panel in part of the card. With a little bit of thought, children can put secret messages into all sorts of different places within the card.

Materials

Art paper

Rulers for measuring

Crayons and markers

Scissors

Adhesives such as glue sticks, or double-sided or clear tape

Procedures

Have the children first plan the overall theme or design of the card and decide if a secret message or object fits the overall theme of the card. For example, if a child is giving a card to a special friend, he or she may want to include instructions for a secret handshake. The instructions for the handshake can be hidden on a piece of paper in a secret compartment of the card.

The children will also need to determine what the secret object or message should be. An object should be flat or not too thick so it will fit easily into the secret compartment. A handle made out of a tiny strip of paper attached to the message or hidden object might help.

There are many places where the secret message or objects can be hidden depending on the design of the card. A small slit, a picture with a small flap, or complicated false panels in the front or back cover are all workable solutions.

Some children may want to include a treasure map or a list of clues to direct the recipient to the hidden objects. The treasure map gives children an opportunity to practice writing instructions. Arrows on the card may be another solution.

Birthday Cards

Some children like to make secret message notes as birthday cards with a special secret birthday message. If the card is going to accompany a present, children could include hints regarding the contents of the package. It is fun to watch the recipient read the card and then try to figure out what the gift is.

Valentines

Secret messages are especially appropriate for valentines.

Appreciation Day Cards

Children may want to hide notes explaining the reasons the person (such as a mother, father, or grandparent) is especially important.

Pop-Up Cards

Cards with an object that pops up when the card is opened fascinate children. These are very similar to books with pop-up pictures. There are two basic types of pop-ups: cut-out pop-ups and extra object pop-ups. Both types can usually be made by children in the second grade and above, but some kindergartners and first and second graders have difficulty manipulating the paper so that the pop-ups actually work.

Cut-Out Pop-Ups

These cards consist of a single object cut out of the base card and inverted so that the shape stands when the card is opened.

Materials

> Construction paper
>
> Scissors
>
> Rulers or straight edges
>
> Pencils, crayons, and markers
>
> Tape

Procedures

Have children determine the overall theme of the card. Children need to consider what kind of object they would like to have pop up. Shapes that have right angles, square corners, and straight lines work well. Seats of chairs, boxes, cages, computer monitors, television screens, and presents also tend to succeed. Objects that have irregular shapes do not stand as well; children should try to avoid hearts, apples, and flowers, all of which work better with extra object pop-ups.

Children should fold the card inside out and then cut out two parallel slits that are perpendicular to the crease or fold of the card. The shape is then forced forward or inverted when the card is opened. When the card is closed, the cut out is folded. Children need to be cautioned that the pop-up object should be able to lie within the edges of the card (Figure 7–2).

Before children make pop-up cards, they should be given opportunities to experiment with the overall construction of pop-ups. Some children will be able to construct pop-ups very easily and will understand the basic concept. Other children, even those in intermediate grades, may not be able to make pop-ups without a great deal of supervision. When the children plan the overall design of the card, they probably need to make a model.

Figure 7–2

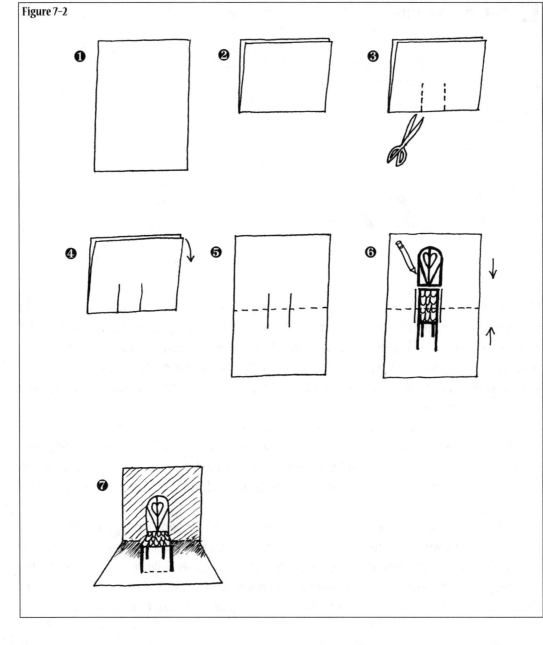

◉ Cage Pop-Ups

One design of pop-ups that children especially enjoy making are cages to house animals. When the card is opened, a three-dimensional cage with animals inside is revealed.

Materials

Scissors

Crayons, markers, and colored pencils

Straight edges or rulers

Construction paper or lightweight cardstock

Clear tape

Glue stick

Optional: String

Optional: Adhesive labels (for making animal stickers)

Procedures

Obviously, cages work best with cards that have an animal theme. Have the children select a piece of colored construction paper or lightweight cardstock for the base card and then a smaller piece of a contrasting color for the cage. For the cage, children should cut a square that is up to 40 percent of the area of the base card. Next, they draw parallel lines to mark the bars of the cage. These lines should be one-quarter inch apart, leaving a quarter-inch margin on all sides of the square. Have the children cut on the lines, leaving the margins untouched.

Next, have children fold the paper in half. Reopen the paper, and fold every other bar inward. Care should be taken so that none of the bars of the cage break (tape can mend any broken bars). Children may need to practice placing the cage so that it is contained within the card when the card is closed.

Once children are satisfied that the cage fits, they glue the cage to the inside of the base card with half of the bars folded inward and the other half folded outward. The open frame of the cage is placed inside the card. Children should hold the card open when they place the cage into the card.

Attach a small paper animal to a piece of string and then fasten the string to one of the top bars of the cage. The children should write the messages for their cards after the cage has been made because they will not know how much room the cage will take up.

◉ Extra Object Pop-Ups

With this type of card, children make a pop-up by attaching an extra object parallel to the card's interior crease or fold. An object is taped at an angle in the card so that when the card is opened, the object pops up. You may also have a couple of students with exceptional problem-solving skills who will be able to come up with their own innovative pop-up designs.

Materials

Construction paper or lightweight cardstock

Scissors

Tape

Crayons, markers, and colored pencils

Procedures

Have the children plan the overall design of the card. They need to consider what kinds of object they want to pop up. With this type of pop-up, the children create an object smaller in size than the card is when closed. This is a challenge for some children.

After the children make an object, they need to carefully fasten it to the center of the card with small pieces of tape. Then they check the card to make sure that it will open and close easily (Figure 7–3).

Figure 7-3

Pocket Notes

Children have a tendency to put all sorts of things into pockets. Although they often forget what went into a pocket, the things children put into their pockets were at least once very important to them! Pocket notes can be integrated into many different card designs.

Materials

Construction paper or cardstock

Scissors

Crayons, markers, pens, and pencils

Straight edges or rulers

Procedures

Have the children plan the overall design and figure out what objects or messages will be placed in pockets. They may want to brainstorm the types of objects that the card recipient likes or wishes to have. Pockets can be all sorts of different types of containers: pots, pans, drawers, cupboards, briefcases, suitcases, purses, wallets, and wastebaskets are all good material (Figure 7–4). They also need to think about where the pocket will be placed in relation to the rest of the illustrations and written messages. Finally, encourage the children to make pockets with seams (a small fold of the paper). Pockets with seams last much longer than pockets without.

Figure 7-4 A pocket card with flowers

Graduation pocket notes are great—especially if children can create their own diplomas for the recipient.

Mobile Cards

Mobiles are fun to make and hang. With a mobile card, a very simple mobile is slipped into two slits in the base card. The top of the mobile is a flat strip, and the hanging objects are attached to it. The recipient should be able to remove the mobile easily. The mobile can be made and placed on the cover, in the interior, or in the message portion of the card.

Materials

Cardstock or heavyweight construction paper

Scissors

String

Markers, crayons, pencils, and pens

Procedures

When designing the mobile card, the children may want to carefully consider how the mobile and the message will work together. They also need to consider what objects they would like to include in the mobile. Colors for the base card and mobile should be carefully chosen to complement one another.

Each piece of the mobile must be measured so it will fit within the perimeter of the base card. The strings are attached to the back of the strip of paper at the top of the mobile. The mobile pieces should be laid on the cover. Then construct the anchor flap. Next, strings that go from the anchor flap to the individual pieces of the mobile should be attached.

Two slits are then placed in the base card. The anchor strip is inserted into the base card with the mobile pieces hanging down. If the individual mobile pieces are too long, the pieces of string can be gently wrapped around the anchor strip. When the mobile is hung, the individual pieces can be unwound.

◉ Get-Well Cards

A mobile can be a cheery gift for ill people. The child may want to write riddles with the question on one side of each suspended item and the answer on the other side.

◉ Invitations

The information section of an invitation can be made out of different parts of a mobile. For example, the date of the event can be listed on one piece, the type of event (such as a party) on another, and so on.

 Pocketbook Cards

Pocketbook cards are a cross between a pocketbook and a greeting card. A pocketbook is drawn freehand and then cut out. A ribbon forms a fine handle for the pocketbook; a greeting on the outside and/or a buckle or other decoration make good additions as well. A message is also written inside a pocketbook.

◉ Materials

Construction paper or cardstock

Scissors

Ribbon, yarn, and string,

Crayons, markers, and pens

◉ Procedures

Children may want to start making a pocketbook card with a list of items the recipient probably carries or would like to carry in a pocketbook. They must decide if a pocketbook card is appropriate for the message. Pictures are often appreciated by mothers.

Have children make the base pocketbook card and then practice opening and closing the card before writing their message. The outside of the card can have the name or initials of the recipient, or simply buckles. The buckles can be made out of pieces of aluminum foil. Once the message has been written onto the card, children can make a strap or handle (Figure 7–5).

Figure 7-5

◉ Briefcase Cards

Briefcase cards are a good alternative to pocketbook cards. The same basic principles of making a pocketbook card are applied for briefcase cards. Instead of making a handle out of ribbon or yarn, children can make the briefcase handle out of construction paper, cardstock, or heavy construction paper.

◉ Appreciation Day Cards

Pocketbook and briefcase cards are especially appropriate for appreciation days such as Mother's Day, Father's Day, Grandparent's Day, or Secretary's Day. These cards provide an opportunity for children to express themselves.

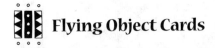 Flying Object Cards

Flying object cards have a scene or picture with a miniature model of a "flying object" attached to the card with a string. There is also a small slit that serves as a perch for the flying object. The flying object can be a real object that flies, such as a kite, bird, airplane, parachute, helicopter, or butterfly, or a fanciful object, such as a dragon, mythical bird, or an angel.

◉ Materials

Construction paper

Markers, crayons, pens, and pencils

Scissors

Masking or clear tape

Heavy thread or fishing line

Optional: Needle and thread

◎ Procedures

If a flying object is appropriate for their occasion or message, the children need to figure out what the flying object should be. It is very difficult to create cards with more than two flying objects because the strings have a tendency to get tangled. The child needs to plan a "perch" for the flying object to sit on when it's not airborne.

When designing the card, the children need to think about how the flying object will be integrated. The flying object can be placed on the cover or in the message section of the card. The flying object in one child's Father's Day card was a TV remote control (Figure 7–6). Children should draw all of the illustrations and write all of the messages for the card. With this particular style of card, it helps to draw a model of the flying object. Students then attach a piece of thread or string to the back of the flying object with a piece of clear tape. The other half of the thread or fishing line can be attached to the base card with a needle and thread or tape. Children who have well-developed perceptual skills often make very sophisticated flying object cards.

Figure 7-6

YOU ARE THE BEST FATHER in the hole world. I LOVE YOU!

HAPPY FATHERS DAY

TV Remote

⊙ Bon Voyage Cards

Flying object cards make great bon voyage cards if the object matches the mode of transportation of the card's recipient.

Designing Envelopes

Envelopes are something that we often take for granted. However, paper and envelope sizes vary from country to country, and many children enjoy looking at envelopes from different countries.

Children can create many types of envelopes. Some like to investigate how the paper is folded and put together; adults can steam and pull apart envelopes for children to examine. Children can replicate these designs and also invent their own envelope styles.

Children are often fascinated with aerograms because the writing paper doubles as an envelope. The price of postage for an aerogram is less than the price of sending a regular airmail letter.

One second grader became very frustrated because her card would not fit into any commercially produced envelopes. She made an envelope that had at least twenty folds and six or seven layers of paper. Her card was lovely, but she was even more proud of the envelope.

⊙ Materials

Paper bags

Photocopier paper

Used large manila, white, or colored envelopes

Scissors

Optional: Wrapping paper for envelope liners

◉ Procedures

There are two basic styles of envelopes. In the basic design, the envelope construction is very square, perhaps with a few rounded edges or corners. The second type is more of a triangular design and is found more frequently in the United States. Show students some samples.

After the children have examined the envelopes, let them design and make their own. Practicing with newspaper is a good idea and helps students form a real sense of how their designs will work.

Envelope Flourishes

The exteriors of envelopes can be decorated with flourishes such as paper doilies, ribbon, stickers, and sequins. Be careful about extras on envelopes destined for the post office.

Many fancy envelopes have liners that can be seen when the flap portion of the envelope is lifted. Liners are inserted in the finished envelopes. They can easily be made out of lightweight wrapping paper; wallpaper is usually too stiff. Liners are especially nice for envelopes with an unsealed and tucked in flap, which enables the recipient to see the liner more readily.

Embedded Envelopes

It is great fun to open up one box and then have another smaller box inside that contains an even smaller box. The same basic concept can be used to make embedded envelope cards and works very well if children want to write a message in parts. Messages written on the envelopes often correspond with the messages written inside each envelope.

◉ Materials

Crayons, markers, and pens

Photocopier paper

Scissors

Paper for making envelopes (i.e. photocopier paper or other types that are easy to fold and will not crack)

◉ Procedures

Have the children write out their entire message and think about the overall design of their card. They need to figure out how they are going to break up their message as well as how each part of the message will be illustrated. It is also important to consider what will be included on the envelopes and on the individual letters.

The children should determine how many envelopes they will need for their project. Since it is often expensive to find envelopes in graduated sizes, children can create their own customized envelopes.

◉ Get-Well Cards

Embedded cards can really brighten up the life of someone who is ill. One child called them "miniature surprise cards."

◉ Birthday Cards

Children can make embedded cards as a substitute for a birthday present. When the recipient has opened up all of the envelopes, he or she is greeted with a special birthday message. Children need to work especially hard on the final greeting to make sure it is meaningful.

◉ Announcements

Embedded envelope cards can make terrific announcements for weddings, the birth of a child, or a graduation. In each envelope, children may include a hint or a clue to help the recipient figure out what is being announced. For example, for a baby announcement, the writer might want to say that something arrived (literally) in the middle of the night.

 **Lace Cards**

Lace cards can be created out of paper doilies or student-made lace. The lace can be attached to the front panel of the card or as the back flap for envelopes that will be hand-delivered. (Lace envelopes cannot be delivered by the postal service as they can easily get caught in the mail-processing machinery.)

Materials

> Paper doilies in white, gold, silver, pink, red or other colors
>
> Construction paper or lightweight cardstock
>
> Clear tape and/or white adhesive removable labels
>
> Glue sticks or white glue
>
> Optional: plastic or cloth tape

Procedures

If lace is appropriate for the type of message a child wishes to send, she or he should consider the overall size of the card. They can use whole doilies or can cut the doilies into pie-shaped pieces. One large doily can be used to create the front panel of the card or the flap of the envelope. An alternative is to attach a number of doilies together to make the cover or flap.

The children probably need to practice putting the pieces of lace together to make sure that everything will fit together. After children have laid out the lace and are satisfied, they can attach each piece of lace with pieces of white adhesive labels or tape.

Once the children are happy with the lace, they are ready to prepare the base card. The base card can be one panel attached to the lace card. Or the lace can be attached to a cover of a base card that opens and closes (Figure 7–7).

Valentine's Day Cards

Children can make the basic lace card or a base card and lace card in the shape of a heart. If only white doilies are available, the lace can be colored with pink markers.

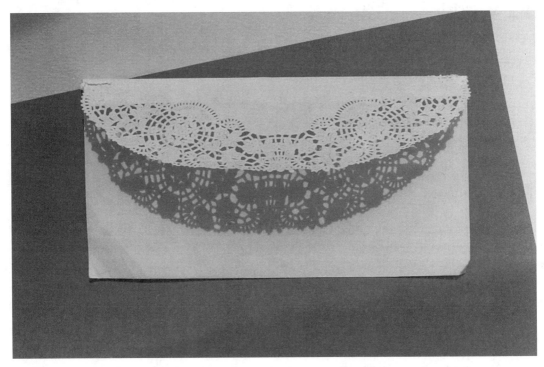

Figure 7-7

The Artist's Perspective

CHAPTER

8

Creating Cards and Writing Paper

All of the techniques described in this chapter work well whether or not they are applied to cards and writing paper. The activities are especially appealing to children who enjoy specific artistic techniques such as painting or flower arranging. There is also some attention paid to calligraphy and other artistic methods of forming letters.

Painting and printmaking cards and writing paper are authentic and purposeful ways for children to explore abstract art. String paintings, cotton swab paintings, sponge paintings, and prints made with objects such as coins or with fingers can cover notecards or adorn writing paper. Once the paint dries, these abstract pieces of art can be cut out and mounted on construction paper or writing paper to create notecards and stationery. Bows made out of yarn or ribbon are an attractive finishing touch for notecards.

Many artistic techniques can be used to decorate children's notecards and writing paper. Most of the ones here involve very simple painting and printmaking strategies. They include:

- Bark painting cards
- String painting cards

- Sponge painting cards

- Cotton swab paintings

- Fingerprint creatures

- Crayon rubbing cards

- Calligraphy and fine penmanship

- Dried flower cards and writing paper

- "Rice paper" cards

- Tissue paper cards

 ## Bark Painting Cards

In Mexico there are many attractive greeting cards made out of bark paper. One of my favorite forms of writing paper, bark paper is handmade from tree bark. It is dark brown and has a rough texture, and designs are painted directly onto the bark paper using brightly colored paint. In many places, glossy cards that contain a photographic reproduction of a real bark paper painting are available.

◉ Materials

Brown paper grocery bags or lunch bags

Colored chalk or pastels

Markers, crayons, pens, and pencils

Photocopier paper for card liners

Optional: hair spray (nonaerosol)

Optional: authentic bark painting cards

⊙ Procedures

Have children think about the types of designs or symbols that would be appropriate for both the occasion and the recipient. The actual bark painting is generally on the cover of the card, and stick figures and other simple objects help give the cards the feeling of bark paintings. In Mexico, the paintings are usually made with very bright colors.

Provide children with brown paper grocery bags or lunch bags. Have children wad or scrunch up the paper bags and then cut out a picture from a bag and mount it to the cover of the base card. Next, the design is drawn on the card.

This type of card is especially appropriate if children are studying Mexico, but variations are found in other Latin American cultures as well.

 String Painting Cards

String paintings are comprised of jagged lines in very vivid colors. String paintings are considered abstract art and are easy enough for even very young children. Older children can experiment with primary colors and color mixing. Children like making these paintings because the final painting is a surprise: they don't know what it will look like until they unfold the paper.

⊙ Materials

String

Different colors of tempera paint

Paper or plastic plates

Photocopier paper

Construction paper or cardstock

Scissors

Glue sticks

Ribbons or yarn

◉ Procedures

Place tempera paint of each color in a plastic or paper plate. Place a string that is approximately six to six-and-one-half inches in length in the paint on each plate. It is helpful to wrap a small piece of clear tape around one end of the string. This makes it easier to find the string once it is covered with paint.

Have children fold a piece of letter-sized paper in half and then open the paper up again. Lift one string out of the paint and let the excess paint drip onto the plate. Place the string on the right side of the paper. Add other strings. Fold the paper over and then gently rub the paper while it is still closed. If children don't want a smeared effect, they should rub the paper in an up-and-down manner. Finally, open the card and remove the strings.

Once the string paintings have dried, the children can cut out their favorite part. They may cut them out in rectangular shapes or in the same design as the painting. A piece of construction paper or cardstock serves as an excellent base card; have children attach the shape to the card. They can finish the card by putting two holes in the fold and attaching string, yarn, or ribbon. The dried string from the painting part of the project can be attached as a final flourish, although some paints will peel or crumble off of the string.

◉ Poems

The paintings and prints can be used as a backdrop for poems or other short pieces of writing. Children write their poem on a small piece of paper and mount it on top of the painting or the print.

◉ Invitations

Painting and printed cards make very appropriate invitations for parents to attend events such as student art exhibits or art auctions to benefit a school. They can also be used for invitations to invite visiting or guest artists to come to a school or classroom.

◉ Permission Slips

These types of cards can be used as a cover for permission slips for a child to participate in a specific event. Children can write the general information about the event on the card. The official permission slip that the parent or guardian needs to sign can be duplicated in advance and inserted into the card.

◉ Notecards

Children may want to make a supply of painting and print cards. Extras can stock the classroom correspondence writing center.

▤ Sponge Painting Cards and Writing Paper

Sponge paintings are created by children dipping sponges into paint and applying them directly to the paper. Sponge paintings can be formed on the cover of a base card or placed directly on the writing paper. Children can also make a sponge painting on a piece of paper that will be mounted on a base card.

◉ Materials

Sponges

Tempera paint

Paper or plastic plates or pie tins

Construction paper or lightweight cardstock

Writing paper

Optional: clamp-style clothespins

 **Procedures**

Place several colors of tempera paint in plastic or paper plates or pie tins. Clothespins can be attached to the sponges to make the process less messy. The children then dip a sponge into the paint and then delicately apply it on paper or on the front of the base card. The process is repeated until the child is satisfied with the finished product.

The children may want to decorate writing paper with a border of sponge painting at the top or bottom of each sheet, or a couple of impressions can be placed in the corners. Matching envelopes look nice.

Let the children experiment with this technique. One kindergartner decided to sponge paint with fall colors and showed a very sophisticated awareness of how colors can be combined.

 Cotton Swab Paintings

Cotton swab paintings are made up of numerous brightly colored tempera paint dots. Cotton swab paintings are made with cotton swabs and tempera paint and can be created by very young children. As a colleague pointed out early in my career, this painting technique gives young children an opportunity to practice using the same small-motor skills that they use to draw and write.

Materials

> Cotton swabs
>
> Small plastic or paper drinking cups or other paint containers
>
> Tempera paint
>
> Small sheets of paper (less than twelve inches in diameter; recycled newsprint works very well)
>
> Construction paper or lightweight cardstock
>
> Writing paper

Glue sticks

Ribbon or yarn

◉ Procedures

Place no more than one inch of tempera paint in each drinking cup, and put one or two cotton swabs next to each cup of paint. Each child will need a sheet of paper. Have children paint with an up-and-down motion. The cotton swabs quickly disintegrate when children rub the paper from side to side. After children have finished painting, they should let the paintings dry. (These paintings sometimes take longer to dry than other paintings because the dots can be very thick.)

When the paintings have dried, have children cut them out and mount them onto base cards. Some children enjoy cutting out a cluster of dots and adding stems for a vase filled with flowers. Other children may wish to decorate the border or top of writing paper.

 Fingerprint Creature Cards

These cards and writing papers are covered with finger- and thumbprint creatures. Working from fingerprints, children draw features such as eyes, ears, noses, and mouths. These cards work especially well when a humorous effect is desired.

◉ Materials

Stamp pads

Soap or premoistened cleansing cloths for cleaning fingers

Construction paper or lightweight cardstock

Writing paper

Fine-tipped markers

Procedures

The children may want to add fingerprint creatures to a note or greeting card to decorate writing. They can make mammals, fish, plants, or other objects with oval shapes brought to life with fine-tipped markers. Speech bubbles can give voice to the creations.

Animal Family Card Collection

Fingerprint animals can be used as the basis for animal stories. Some children may want to make an entire line of cards based on one fingerprint animal family. Each card can describe a different aspect of the animal family's life.

Crayon Rubbing Cards

Attractive cards and writing paper can be made with crayon rubbings. An object such as a leaf, key, coin, or comb is placed under a sheet of paper and then the flat side of a crayon is used to make an impression of the object on top of the card. Leaves and dried grasses make cards that nature lovers will enjoy.

Materials

Crayons or colored pencils

Lightweight paper

Objects for rubbings (e.g., real lace doilies, coins, leaves, dried weeds)

Optional: construction paper or cardstock

Procedures

Let each child select a flat but textured object that is meaningful to the recipient. The actual rubbing should be done on lightweight paper so there is a clear impression. If necessary, it can be cut out and mounted on the base card. Some children may want to decorate writing paper or envelopes with more than one rubbing.

Calligraphy and Fine Penmanship

Calligraphy and cursive writing are no longer widely used. Fancy penmanship is very artistic, and there are many different types of cursive writing from around the world.

Calligraphy Writing

In recent years, calligraphy has become more popular, and specialized pens and books make calligraphy easier. Calligraphy styles for printing and cursive writing are available.

Materials

> Calligraphy pens
>
> Writing paper
>
> Optional: An experienced calligrapher

Procedures

Invite a calligraphy artist to your classroom to share techniques with children. Writing their names is a great way to begin learning. Good calligraphy requires time and patience. I usually urge children to only start using calligraphy for key words; the bulk of their message is written in simpler types of handwriting.

◉ Cursive or Fancy Handwriting

Many different cultures view handwriting as an art. Fancy handwriting can be a bridge toward calligraphy. Although computers are frequently used for personal writing, many children enjoy exploring the art of handwriting. Forming letters can be a means of self-expression.

Materials

Different writing instruments

Samples of cursive writing

Different types of paper

Optional: a talented cursive writer

Procedures

You may wish to invite someone known for beautiful penmanship to come to your class. Children may want to experiment with felt-tipped pens, ballpoint pens, fountain pens, or even quill pens. Have children practice writing different messages such as "Happy Birthday" using various handwriting styles. Supply several kinds of paper as well.

If students are studying about European cultures, they may want to look at different examples of fine penmanship from Europe.

◉ Character Painting

Learning to form characters with brushes is considered an art in many cultures, especially in Asian cultures. Some children may be familiar with character writing and can serve as class experts. Your students may choose to learn a few characters or a name to integrate into their cards.

Materials

Writing brushes

Ink

Examples of Asian-language characters

Writing paper

Optional: An expert on some type of traditional Asian character writing

Procedures

If at all possible, invite someone to your class who can write with Asian characters. In China and Japan, characters are an important part of the written language. Some systems also have phonetic characters (such as Hebrew and Korean), and Chinese characters are often an important part of the written languages elsewhere in Asia. Encourage your children to copy characters they like or to make up their own.

If children are studying an Asian culture that has a character-based written language, they may wish to learn how to sign their name. The phonetic characters of Japanese and Korean alphabets work well for this. Your children will discover that not all sounds in English exist in Japanese or Korean.

Dried Flower Cards and Writing Paper

In many Eastern European countries, dried flower cards are considered a folk art. These cards combine the arts of flower arranging and flower drying and have a lovely and gentle feel to them.

Materials

Fresh or predried flowers

Heavyweight construction paper or lightweight cardstock

Heavy books (such as dictionaries) for flower pressing, or a flower press

Crayons, markers, and pens

White glue

Toothpicks

Clean newsprint

Optional: books about flower drying, flower pressing, and/or flower arranging

◉ Procedures

Have children select flowers they would like to include in cards. Allow fresh flowers to air-dry for several hours so they are not too moist. Small flowers, such as forget-me-nots and violets, work very well, as do individual petals from daisies, pansies, and roses. Place the flowers or individual petals on sheets of clean blank newsprint or white pieces of paper. Newspapers cannot be used to press flowers because the ink is easily transferred onto the flowers. Place a second sheet of blank newsprint or white paper on top of the flowers, topped by several heavy books for weight. If you have access to one, a flower press also works well.

Allow flowers to dry three to four days until firm. Next, have children select a color of cardstock or construction paper for the base card. Let the children practice laying flowers on colored pieces of paper until they find the perfect color for the base card. Be sure to allow the children an opportunity to practice with artistic flower arrangements before they attach the flowers to the card. Some children may prefer to wait to fix the flowers to their card until after they have written their message. Once the flowers are on the base card, it is very difficult to make any changes in the message. It is much easier to rewrite a message than to put new flowers on the cover.

When children are satisfied with their message, have the children decide where to place the flowers on the cover. Toothpicks are good tools to apply the glue and keep the covers neat. After removing the flowers from the trial placement, dip the toothpick into the white glue and lightly paint the surface. Next, gently attach a flower or a petal to the card (Figure 8–1). Once completed, carefully store the card until it is delivered. Writing paper also benefits from one or two dried flowers. These cards are especially appropriate if children are studying about ecosystems, plants, or animals. Children can write some information about their flowers on the back panel of the card.

Figure 8-1 Latvian dried flower cards

Sympathy Cards, Wedding Cards, Appreciation Day Cards, Anniversary Cards, Birth Announcement Cards

Flower cards are appropriate for all occasions when flowers might be sent. The students might want to look at floral catalogs and think about what types of flowers are associated with specific events.

"Rice Paper" Cards

"Rice paper" cards have an Asian feel to them, and this is an appropriate project if you are studying Asian cultures. You can simulate rice paper with waxed paper, which is then placed into a frame to make the cover of the card. I first learned of this technique from my mother when I was a small child.

Materials

      Waxed paper

      Small leaves or flowers

      Construction paper or lightweight cardstock

      Household iron

      Optional: authentic rice paper

Procedures

When planning the overall design of the card, remember that the rice paper is best used as the cover of a card. The children initially need to decide how large they want their base card to be, preferably made with construction paper or lightweight cardstock. A frame for the rice paper is cut from the base card cover. Remind students to ignore the message portion of the card as they cut.

      Gather small and skinny items such as small leaves to be placed in the "rice paper." Arrange the items in an artistic manner on top of a sheet of wax paper, which has been trimmed to the size of the cover. Put a second sheet of rice paper on top of the first and bring the wax-paper sandwich to an area set up for ironing. Children should not handle or stand near the iron. Be sure to have a parent or other adult use the iron. After the objects and paper have been ironed together, attach this "rice paper" to the card's frame.

 **Tissue Paper Cards**

Colored tissue paper and either liquid starch or watered-down white glue can form an attractive picture. These cards help children develop a sense of color.

◎ Materials

> Colored tissue paper
>
> Liquid starch or white glue
>
> Plastic or paper plates
>
> Construction paper or lightweight cardstock.

◎ Procedures

To plan the design of the card, the children need to select the colors of tissue paper and consider how the colors will look when they are put together. Certain colors may best fit the message of the card. Have children make a base card out of construction paper or lightweight construction paper.

Once the base card has been made, provide children with tissue paper and the liquid starch or a glue-and-water mixture. After tearing up pieces of tissue paper, carefully dip one piece at a time into the adhesive . Press off excess liquid with your fingers and place the tissue paper on the base card. Repeat this process until satisfied with the overall effect.

◎ Valentine's Day Cards

If children are writing Valentine's Day notes, they may want to use pink, red, and white tissue paper. Children can cut out the pink and red tissue paper in the shape of hearts to enhance the effect.

◎ Autumn Holiday Cards

For holidays and events such as Halloween, Thanksgiving, and starting back to school, your children may want to make cards using fall colors. Children can cut out the tissue paper in the shape of autumn leaves before they put them on the cover.

Notes for Fun

My students and I like to make things. We feel successful when we have created something attractive and intriguing. The projects in this chapter can best be considered crafts. They lend themselves to problem solving and discovery and don't require much artistic talent. Most fit very easily into an elementary school program, but they have also succeeded with older learners and with children at home. I have tried to include projects that only require very simple supplies found in most classrooms and homes. A few of the projects, however, require adult assistance and supervision.

The projects discussed in this chapter include:

- Doorknob notes
- Marbled paper
- Scratch-and-sniff notes
- Recycled materials cards
- Humble pie cards

- Aged paper
- "Please write back!" notecards
- Stamps and seals

 ## Doorknob Notes

Children are especially drawn to objects that belong to the world of adults. One of the simplest ways of publishing children's correspondence is to make doorknob notes. The "Do Not Disturb" and "Please Clean This Room" signs found in hotels and motels are perhaps the most familiar type of doorknob notes. Children especially like the two-sided format of doorknob notes. Children creating a message on one side often will keep peeking at the other side to see if both sides really go together.

Doorknob signs in hotels and motels take diverse approaches; some are written in two languages, on laminated cardstock, or with pictures or other graphics. Many of them have a company logo. You might want to collect and display a variety of these signs.

Materials

Construction paper or lightweight cardstock (for younger children)

Heavier cardstock (for older students)

Scissors

Procedures

Each note consists of an oblong or oval piece of paper with a hole at one end so it can be hung on a doorknob (Figure 9–1). Young children can use construction paper or lightweight cardstock that can be cut with school scissors. Older students may prefer heavier cardstock and sharper scissors.

Figure 9-1 Not all correspondence is kind and sweet. This message reads, "Don't bug me."

Some children enjoy having professional doorknob signs as patterns for their own notes. In theory, I prefer to have children resist the urge to use a pattern and to "eyeball" the outline of the note freehand, which encourages problem solving. I don't mind having different lids available as patterns for the circle.

The children will need to consider how big the doorknob hole should be. If the hole is too big, it may tear easily. They also need to be aware of how close the hole should be to the top edge of the note, how to make the hole perfectly round, and how to construct the note so that it will not be crooked when it hangs. In many classrooms, there isn't always enough time for children to experiment with the construction of the doorknob note. Be sure to set aside some time.

Doorknob notes are fun to deliver. Youngsters can discuss the best method and time of delivery. I also like to have children report on how the delivery went, how long it took for the recipient to discover the note, and the recipient's reaction.

Mother's Day, Father's Day, Grandparent's Day Cards

Awards or certificate cards for the best parent, grandparent, friend, brother, or sister are popular doorknob notes. Beginning ESL students or writers might try a simple description or biography award. Some students may also like to draw a picture or make a collage illustrating the person or simply listing the qualities that earned the recipient the award.

◎ Bilingual Cards

Doorknob notes work well when children want to create bilingual cards, writing the same message in a different language on each side. If children want to include poems on their bilingual cards, it's best if they can be shown how to translate the spirit of the poem and not just the individual words.

◎ Thank-You Notes

When children receive a special present, they often like to say thank you with a doorknob note because these have a certain permanence and prominence. Sometimes children like to include a photograph or a hand-drawn picture of the present.

◎ Birthday Cards

Children enjoy making birthday doorknob notes for family members living in the same household with them. The notes can be created and delivered before the birthday person wakes up. Riddle birthday cards—with the riddle on one side and the answer on the other—work especially well.

 **Marbled Paper**

There are many fancy techniques for creating marbled paper. I discovered a homier version when I was teaching young children in northern California. It is amazingly simple, requiring only waxed crayons, vegetable peelers, vegetable graters, and a household iron (Figure 9–2). This activity can be set up as a learning center staffed by a parent volunteer or teacher's aide.

Figure 9-2 Pictorial instructions for making marbled paper.

◎ Materials

Waxed crayons (old, short crayons work well)

Vegetable or cheese grater, vegetable peeler, or crayon sharpener

Crayons or markers

Household iron

Photocopier paper

Newspaper

Optional: empty egg cartons or muffin tins

◎ Procedures

Grate the crayons with vegetable peelers or graters. Plastic cheese graters are generally safer than metal ones, but with all graters children must watch their fingers. They may want to wear plastic or latex gloves to protect their fingers. The crayon shavings are put into egg cartons or muffin tins according to color.

Next, pick up a piece of white paper and sprinkle three quarters of a teaspoon of shavings on top, radiating out from the center of the page. Then put another sheet of white paper on top to create a paper-crayon-paper sandwich.

Bring the paper sandwich to an area set up for ironing. A teacher or another adult should operate the iron while children watch from a safe distance. Put the crayon sandwich on top of several sheets of newspaper and an additional sheet of newspaper on top of the crayon sandwich. Set the iron at medium-low and rub the sandwich for four to ten seconds—until the crayon has melted and bled through the paper. When the sandwich is taken apart, two lovely pieces of matching marbled paper are revealed.

The marbled paper can be cut out and then mounted on a piece of paper to make a greeting card (Figure 9–3). Encourage children to mount the marbled paper on a color that shows off the design.

This is a good activity for children to experiment with primary and secondary colors.

Figure 9-3 Marbled paper

You may want to help them discover which primary colors can be combined to form different secondary colors. Children quickly discover which colors when put together turn into a mudlike color.

Marbled paper is very well suited for almost any personal note or letter and has the feeling of fancy stationery. Each child may want to make a set of ten or twelve marbled paper notecards to have on hand for different personal correspondence projects. In addition, some children may want to make a number of marbled paper cards to stock a correspondence writing center.

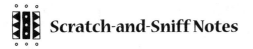 ## Scratch-and-Sniff Notes

Scratch-and-stiff notes are very appealing to students of all ages and are remarkably easy to make. An aromatic food extract or inexpensive cologne is dabbed on a portion of the card. When it dries and the area is scratched, the fragrance is released.

◉ Materials

Aromatic food extracts (e.g. mint, lemon, chocolate, orange, almond, and so on) or inexpensive colognes

Cotton swabs

Construction paper or cardstock

Markers or crayons

Plastic bags or envelopes

◉ Procedures

Ask the children to plan the design and message of the card. Have them make the greeting cards with one space, approximately one inch in diameter, reserved for the fragrance. The fragrance can be placed on the interior or exterior covers or message portion. (The odor cannot be placed over waxed crayon but will work fine when it is dabbed over paper colored with markers.) Then students should identify a scent on hand that they would like to use.

Have children draw a circle indicating the place for the scent. Apply the fragrance to the space indicated with a cotton swab. They should also write instructions telling the recipient of the card where to scratch to release the fragrance. This is important because the area where the scent was applied will be invisible after it dries.

When students have completed the card, they should let it dry for a couple of minutes. Once it is completely dry, the card should be put in a tight-fitting envelope or a plastic bag. For a month or more, the scent will last if the card is sealed.

◉ Winter Holiday Greetings

Many colognes for men have wintry scents such as pine or nutmeg, which could enhance winter holiday cards. Your students may also want to include poems about winter, proverbs for the coming year, and even New Year's resolutions.

Invitations

Food fragrances are fun for invitations for events where food will be served; chocolate is one of the most popular extracts. Some children may want to include the menu for the event or a recipe for one of the dishes as an insert for the card.

Valentine's Day, Birthdays, and Mother's Day Cards

Children can write very flowery messages for different types of greeting cards. Poems and other descriptive writing about flowers, nature, and gardens are especially appropriate. These messages may be illustrated with pictures of flowers or gardens. To finish the card, children can add a floral-scented cologne.

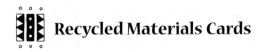 ## Recycled Materials Cards

Some very attractive cards can be made out of discarded materials such as old magazines, newspapers, buttons, and pieces of fabric. A portion of a correspondence learning center can easily be devoted to recycled materials for cards.

Magazine and Newspaper Cards

The covers of these cards have newspaper print or magazine print or illustrations. Each card is lined with used photocopier paper that has one blank side.

Materials

> Old newspapers (sections such as sports, living, business, food, the want-ads, and movies work well)
>
> Old magazines (good topics are sports, women's fashion, home improvement)

Used letter-sized paper (with printing just on one side)

Used twine, string, yarn, or ribbon

Glue sticks

Markers and crayons

Scissors

Pencils

Optional: newspapers and magazines written in different languages

Procedures

Have children plan the design and consider what images or text would be the most appropriate for the design. For example, one child decided that the stock market quotation page fit the theme for a thank-you card for a gift of money.

◎ Recycled School Notices as Writing Paper

A number of years ago, I corresponded with someone in Samoa who wrote his letters on the back of school notices and calendars. This type of correspondence really gave me a sense of the school system and Samoan culture. Leftover notices, newsletters, and calendars all make potentially great stationery.

Materials

Recent school notices with one blank side (e.g. announcements for special events, back-to-school nights, and school picnics, or monthly calendars or school newsletters)

Pens, pencils, markers, or crayons

Procedures

Ask the children to plan their message, considering who will be receiving the message and what the content will be. They may even want to write several drafts.

Next, have the children go through leftover notices and select one that may be especially interesting or that relates to the overall content of their message. The children then write their letter on the blank side. They may want to comment on the notice in their letter. For, example, if they write on a school calendar, they might want to indicate which events they attended and enjoyed.

◉ Discarded Materials Cards

These cards challenge students (and teachers) to reuse products that are not normally considered to have much potential as stationery. They are made almost entirely out of used materials.

Materials

> A wide variety of used materials including but not limited to buttons, ribbon, string, yarn, old tokens, coins in small denominations from other countries, old plane ticket stubs, buckles, cloth flowers, sequins, and bows
>
> School glue, tape, gluesticks, or other safe adhesives
>
> Used file folders, clean and empty very lightweight boxes, or large envelopes

Procedures

Using discarded and recycled materials demands that children think about the weight of the items they want to include. Some heavier materials, for instance, are very difficult to attach to cards. Also, weighty cards will require additional postage. If children are delivering their correspondence by hand, of course, postage is not an issue.

Children may want to write and send Earth Day cards to one another or to groups or individuals who are helping to protect the environment. Children will want to indicate that these cards have been constructed out of recycled materials.

When children write a letter of complaint, they may choose to "recycle" some items that are representative of the product or service that deserves a complaint. For example, if children are objecting to the quality of goods from a candy manufacturer, they may want to include a candy wrapper as a decoration or as an integral part of the content of the card.

◉ Wrapping Paper and Wallpaper Cards

Beautiful notecards and greeting cards can be formed from used wrapping paper and wallpaper. A scrap of wrapping paper lends itself to notecards because only a small piece is needed.

Materials

> Wallpaper sample books
>
> Wrapping paper
>
> Glue sticks
>
> Scissors
>
> Construction paper or lightweight cardstock
>
> Ribbons, string, or yarn

Procedures

Have children select a piece of wrapping paper or wallpaper and a corresponding piece of construction paper or cardstock to frame the former. After making a base card, cut out the wallpaper or wrapping paper so that it is smaller than the base card. Some children like to use the base card as a self-made tracing pattern for the wrapping paper or wallpaper. The children then cut out the wrapping paper an inch or two smaller than the traced pattern. A bow can be attached to the card as a decoration.

Thank-You Notes

Some children may find it fun to use the same wrapping paper from a gift they have received to make a thank-you note.

All-Purpose Notecards

Notecards can be made out of wallpaper and wrapping paper in advance and placed in the learning center or kept in an individual student's desk for future use.

Envelopes

If the cards are going to be hand-delivered, some children may want to make an envelope out of matching wallpaper or wrapping paper. Children can use blank adhesive labels for the recipient's name.

Matching Gift Wrap Cards

If the card is going to accompany a separate gift, children may wish to use the same wrapping paper or wallpaper that covered the gift for the card.

Humble Pie Cards

The idea for this card came from a child who wanted to write an apology for hitting his brother. This type of card is specifically for sending an apology. Paper pie shapes that have been doubled over create the turnover effect of this card

◉ Materials

Ivory-colored cardstock, photocopier paper, or heavy-weight newsprint

Crayons, markers, and pens

Scissors

Optional: Paper to line the card

◉ Procedures

After the children plan their cards, have them draw and cut out an outline of a pie. Next, they should place their fingers on the inside of the rim, pointing outward. They should trace the outlines of their fingers to create a scalloped edge. This is similar to crimping a pie crust.

Children like to make the scallops that give this card a real pie effect. Some children enjoy filling their humble pie with different sweet or meat "fillings"—a lining can be made out of paper to look like a lemon- or banana cream pie filling. The message is then written on a separate piece of paper and pasted on top of the lining.

These cards are intended specifically for apologies. Children can make humble pie notes when they wish to write an apology to someone such as a friend or teacher. I have found that a written apology it is more heartfelt than an oral "I'm sorry."

Some children need extra help to articulate their apology in writing. It may be helpful for children to create the humble pie card as a prewriting activity before they draft the card.

 **Aged Paper**

These papers and cards have an old, almost nostalgic feeling to them. Children can make aged-paper cards using instant coffee, water, and a brush.

 Materials

> Paint brushes or sponges
>
> Regular-strength, instant, or stale coffee
>
> White photocopier paper or butcher paper (some types of cardstock and construction paper can be used)
>
> Matches
>
> Household iron

Procedures

Place one-half cup of regular-strength, instant, or stale coffee into a painting container. Have the children dip a paintbrush or small sponge into the coffee and apply it to a small piece of paper to see if it is absorbed. With a very light touch, the children should apply the coffee to the paper. Set out the paper to dry in a clean, dust-free place. If children want a yellower tint, the paper should be placed in the sun.

Adult volunteers may singe the sides of these cards to create an old "treasure map" appearance. The cards can be singed by placing a match near, but not on, the edge of the card. Also, a very hot iron can singe the sides of some paper. Note that paper singeing should always be done by adults!

You may experiment with painting pieces of photocopier paper and running them through a printer with an old-fashioned font. Some computer printers work better with completely flat and dry aged paper. Other printers work best with aged paper that has been wadded up and flattened out after it has been painted and dried.

Older children may wish to write messages with old-fashioned handwriting. They can also look at correspondence written long ago to learn about how people expressed themselves in the past.

Children can use this paper for writing notes, cards, or letters. Sometimes the paper is very stiff after it has been painted with coffee. For cards, the aged paper should be cut out and mounted onto a base card. The aged paper can also be used as writing paper. Some paper should be placed in a writing center for future use.

"Please Write Back!" Note Cards

When young children write a friendly note or letter to someone, they often expect an instant response. You can ease their concern by having them make two notecards, one with a message and the other left blank. A self-addressed, stamped envelope is included with the blank card that the recipient can use to write back.

Materials

Construction paper, lightweight cardstock, and other notecard supplies

Envelopes

Removable sticky labels

Markers, crayons, and colored pencils

 Procedures

Many of the projects found in this book can be used for "Please write back!" notecards. Have the children make two note cards, with one a little larger than the other. They will also need one envelope for each card. I suggest they write their message on the larger card, along with instructions for the recipient to write back using the smaller card and envelope.

◉ Invitations

Children can include an RSVP or reply card and envelope along with an invitation to a party. Some children may not be familiar with RSVP cards. RSVP is an acronym for the French phrase "Répondez-vous s'il vous plaît," which means "please reply." In many social circles, RSVP cards are used to let a host or hostess know whether or not the individual who has been invited to an event will be able to attend. Many children are interested to know that this helps the hostess or host plan the right amount of food.

⬚ Stamps and Seals

Children can make stamps for envelopes that they will hand-deliver, while seals attached to the back of an envelope can be sent through the mail.

◉ Materials

Adhesive labels or stickers

Markers, crayons, and colored pencils

Scissors

Optional: canceled stamps and stickers or seals

⊙ Procedures

When the children have created a note, card, or letter, they should consider how the correspondence will be delivered. If the correspondence will be hand-delivered, they might want to design their own stamp. If the correspondence will be sent through the U.S. mail, they can make a seal, which is usually placed in the lower left-hand front corner of the envelope or on the back envelope closure.

Encourage children to brainstorm different stamps and seals that would be appropriate for their correspondence. Some children enjoy making their own versions of the "love" stamp series. Celebrity stamps are also popular choices.

CHAPTER 10

Cards That Double as Gifts

There are many times when a card is not quite enough for a specific occasion and you may also want to prepare a gift. Gift cards are simply cards that have a small present as an integral part of the card. For example, if a child creates a card around a reading theme for a friend who loves to read, it would be very logical to include a bookmark as part of the card design. Gift cards provide children with an opportunity to learn the joy of giving.

Many stationery and card manufacturers produce special gift cards, and some of the projects described in this chapter were inspired by commercially available products. You may wish to look at store-bought gift cards for more ideas.

Gift cards work particularly well for appreciation days such as Grandparent's Day or Teacher's Day. They can also be used as birthday cards or valentines. Whether a child prepares a gift or a card for someone often depends upon the relationship that the child has with the recipient, and children seem to appreciate being given the options of putting together a card, gift, or gift card. A gift card is usually easier for kids to create than a gift and a card. In some cases, you may want to have children create their own versions of a particular project for a specific appreciation day, or you might want to set out several projects and let children

decide which gift card they will pursue. These cards take a great deal of preplanning. Not all specific occasions lend themselves to gift cards. In some cases, it is more appropriate to make a gift and a card. If the occasion is suitable, children need to consider the intention of the card, the overall design, and how their written message will make the card complete. The message can be as short as a proverb or as long as several paragraphs. Children should be encouraged to design the card so that the gift and the message work together as a whole.

The projects in this chapter include:

- Bookmark cards
- Sticker-laden cards
- Picture puzzle cards
- Word puzzle cards
- Teapot cards
- Magnet gift cards
- Decorative pins
- Flower baskets
- Activity gift cards
- African proverb necklaces
- Fan cards

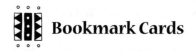 **Bookmark Cards**

Some commercially produced cards include bookmarks as gifts because they can easily be mailed as part of the card; often no additional postage is needed. Bookmarks are an especially nice gift because they encourage literacy. In addition, the child doesn't have to know very much about the recipient. The bookmarks should be incorporated into the cover or message portion of the card (Figure 10–1).

Figure 10-1 A get-well bookmark card

There is a wide variety of bookmarks available for sale. Some consist entirely of pictures. Some have a picture on one side and a written message on the other. Some are humorous, while others are serious or even educational. Rectangles, ovals, and triangles work. Commercially produced bookmarks are usually laminated or made out of heavy plastic or lightweight cardboard.

◎ Materials

Wallpaper samples, lightweight cardstock, and old file folders

Construction paper, old lightweight plastic placemats, contact paper, gift bags, and lightweight boxes

Scissors

Markers (permanent markers are necessary if children will be working on surfaces that resist ink)

Optional: handmade and commercially produced bookmarks

◎ Procedures

Allow the children to select the materials that they will be using to create the bookmarks, only providing materials that children can easily cut with scissors they ordinarily use. Children may need to be reminded to select durable materials so that their gift will last a long time.

Have children plan the overall design of the card: What shape should their bookmark be? How will the bookmark fit into the design? Should there be a message on the bookmark as well as a message on the card?

There should be two horizontal slits in the card so that children can easily insert the bookmark into the exterior cover, interior cover, or message portion of the card. There should be two parallel slots in the base card, with one toward the top of the card. The other should be lower so that the bookmark will easily fit into the cover.

I find that it helps when children make a draft of the bookmark and card to practice cutting out the bookmark and making sure it fits easily. It also helps when children draft any messages that they will use on the bookmark and the card; sometimes they have trouble making sure that the message fits onto the bookmark.

Bookmarks can be laminated or covered with clear contact paper for durability. Children have fun adding embellishments such as tassels, bits of lace, or ribbons.

 Bilingual Bookmarks

Some children may wish to create bilingual bookmarks. Kids can write a message or key word in their primary or native language on one side of the bookmark and a translation or a picture illustrating the message on the other side. Bilingual bookmarks don't have to be given to individuals who speak the same languages as the child. When they give the bookmarks to people who don't speak the same language, it is important to include context clues so that the recipients can figure out the meaning of the words.

Sticker-Laden Cards

Children adore stickers and have been known to beg, scrounge, hunt, and even save money to obtain them. Blank adhesive labels make fine stickers. With a little bit of planning, several stickers can be created, with the stickers and the backing sheet attached to the card.

Young children especially want to give a sticker card to everyone for every occasion. They feel that since they love stickers so much, all recipients will be equally delighted with the gift. Sometimes, when I am trying to get across the concept of audience, I ask children if they know if their parents will love stickers as much as they do. At other times, I just let my students enjoy being givers without having to worry about the genuine reaction of the recipients.

Materials

Markers, crayons, and colored pencils

Blank adhesive labels, preferably in an assortment of sizes

Clear double-sided tape

Construction paper or lightweight cardstock

◎ Procedures

The children need to decide whether the removable stickers will be part of the cover or placed inside the card. Actually, any and all parts of the card can be covered with removable stickers. They can be attached as a single sheet, or several sheets can be integrated into the overall design. One child made a get-well card for another child far along the road to recovery. The cover of the card was an apple tree, and each apple was a removable sticker. The message inside said, "An apple a day keeps the doctor away."

The children should begin construction by making the base card. They may create several drafts before they are ready to add the removable stickers. The stickers can be decorated with pictures, words, or both. The children should also make a draft of the stickers on regular paper before they mark the adhesive labels. Once the children are satisfied with the drafts of the base card and stickers, they can make the final version.

Children may need to be reminded that both the backing sheet and the stickers must be attached to the card. They are fastened with double-sided tape. It is easier if the double-sided tape is first joined to the card and then to the backing sheet.

◎ Children's Cards

Sticker cards are especially appropriate when children want to make gifts for one another as birthday cards, valentines, get-well cards, and bon voyage cards. An entire class can put individual sticker cards together to make a sticker card book as a bon voyage or a get-well gift. Sticker cards are especially appropriate for children who have a cast for a broken bone. The recipient of the sticker card can then place the stickers on the cast.

 **Picture Puzzle Cards**

A picture puzzle with a card can be a big surprise. The puzzle can be displayed anywhere on the card. Children can cut out their picture in interlocking shapes or simply mark the cut lines without actually separating the pieces, allowing the recipient to cut them out later (Figure 10–2). In either case, I've found that the puzzle insert is best included in the card with a plastic sleeve or by adding a small pocket.

Figure 10-2 Puzzle thank-you note—"Thanks a million"

⊙ Materials

Heavyweight paper or lightweight cardstock

Scissors

Markers and crayons

Optional: double-sided tape

Optional: clear plastic for a puzzle sleeve

⊙ Procedures

Encourage children to think about what type of illustration would be the most appropriate for the card. Remind children that their illustrations will be cut into small pieces, and some lend themselves to being cut into smaller pieces better than others. Generally speaking, intricate designs do not look good as puzzle pieces.

There are several different ways to include the puzzle. One way is to attach each puzzle piece to the card using tiny pieces of double-sided tape. Another is to secure the pieces with doubled-sided tape to a backing card, which is then put into a pocket somewhere on the card. A third way is to mount the puzzle without separating the pieces. This requires that the recipient cuts the puzzle apart.

Be sure to encourage the children to think about how the message and the picture will work together. When they are preparing the illustration and making the card, they need to leave enough space for the message.

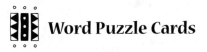

Word Puzzle Cards

Manipulative word puzzles have scrambled words that the recipient must put in the correct order. Younger children usually make word puzzle cards with just one sentence, but older children are capable of writing longer messages that are several sentences or paragraphs in length.

Materials

> Paper
>
> Scissors
>
> Markers and crayons
>
> Optional: double-sided tape
>
> Optional: word-processing program and printer with different fonts

Procedures

To create word puzzles, begin by writing and editing the message and then planning the design of the card, including where the puzzle will be placed. There are several different ways of scrambling word puzzles: by scrambling individual letters in a word, individual words, or individual sentences in one or more paragraphs. Children with strong literacy skills may be able to combine two or three types on the same card.

The puzzle can be attached with tiny pieces of double-sided tape or placed in a pocket. Another approach is to include an additional page with all of the letters or words mixed up so that the recipient must cut apart the individual letters or words and put them back together in the correct order.

Word puzzle cards are appropriate for most occasions, but they work especially well as a gift card for children recuperating from an illness or moving away. They can also be given to adults who love word puzzles.

 Teapot Cards

Teapot cards include a tea bag and instructions to the recipient (usually an adult) to sit and rest and have a cup of tea.

⊙ Materials

    Scrap paper
    Colored paper
    Scissors
    Pencils, markers, and crayons
    Tea bags with strings
    Optional: a teapot or pictures of a teapot, adhesive labels

⊙ Procedures

There are two different types of teapot cards that kids can make. An open-faced or one-sided card has only one illustrated side and no interior; it is shaped like a teapot and has a message and a tea bag. The second type also contains a message and a tea bag, but it opens and closes. The second type is more challenging because it is harder to create a teapot with the edge of the pot on the fold on the left side so that the card opens and closes properly.

Provide the children with scrap paper and pencils, markers, and crayons. It is helpful to have real teapots or pictures of teapots to look at. Have the children practice drawing teapots. After they have some proficiency, ask them to decide which type of card they want to put together. Have children make the card, write the instructions and a message, and then attach a tea bag. Children may want to write a proverb—"A penny saved is a penny earned" or "Don't put all your eggs in one basket"—on the tag of the tea bag.

Children will need a small label for the proverb to cover the existing writing on the tag. Trace the outline of the tag on the label and then cut it out. Next, write a proverb on the label, peel off the backing, and attach it to the tag.

⊙ Multicultural Variations

You may want to have children give teas that represent their own or other cultural backgrounds. For example, many Asians drink green tea, and many Hispanics drink chamomile or hibiscus tea. Speciality teas are frequently available in larger supermarkets or ethnic stores.

 **Magnet Gift Cards**

Baker's clay, felt, fabric, plastic, and papier-mâché can all be used to fashion ornaments that are then attached to small magnets. Magnetic tape is an inexpensive type of magnet available in most hardware stores; it is very easy to work with. Small magnets can also be purchased at hardware stores and variety stores. A steel paper clip fastened to the card holds the magnet. The materials for the different types of ornamental magnets are listed with each project.

◉ Materials

Heavyweight paper or lightweight cardstock

Markers and crayons

Magnetic tape or glue and small magnets, steel paper clips

◉ Procedures

Have children design a card with an integrated magnet. As in other cards, it is important for the message, gift, and card to work together as a whole. The children should make a draft copy of their card and written message. It is important to decide how the magnet will be joined to the card. The paper clip and magnet can be placed on the cover or message area; the magnet cannot be placed on the interior cover because the paper clip will show through on the exterior.

Of course, the children will need to figure out what type of magnetic ornament to make. They may want to think about where the magnet will be placed—a metal filing cabinet, bookshelf, lunch box, lamp, refrigerator, radio, or television. All make good choices. This decision will depend upon the different types of materials available as well as time constraints. Part of the message may be a list of places in the recipient's home or office where the magnet could be hung.

When making the ornaments, children should try to limit the size to no thicker than one-quarter inch (one-eighth inch is better). They should also strive to keep the ornament no wider than one inch in diameter. Most magnets will not be able to hold up a large ornament.

Instructions for making different types of ornamental magnets follow. You may set up several learning centers for a number of varieties.

◉ Baker's Clay Ornaments

Baker's clay is often used to make small ceramic figurines, but it can be made into almost any shape. Kids especially enjoy the medium's flexibility.

Materials

> White flour (not self-rising)
>
> Salt
>
> Water
>
> Mixing bowl
>
> Mixing spoons
>
> Lightly greased baking sheet
>
> Oven or other place to bake ornaments
>
> Tempera paint or markers

Procedures

Mix thoroughly four parts flour with two parts salt and two parts water. You can do this in advance or with the children, but if you make it beforehand, be sure to store the baker's clay in an airtight container such as a plastic bag.

Explain that the class is going to make baker's clay ornaments. Have the children draw a small square or circle that is roughly one inch in diameter on some scratch paper so they can make sure each ornament is not too large. This will become their working surface. Give each child about one tablespoon of baker's clay. Have children make an ornament that is less than one-quarter inch thick and that fits into their outline. An adult should place the sculpted ornaments on a very clean but lightly greased cookie sheet and bake at 350 degrees. Check the oven after ten minutes and continue checking the ornaments at short intervals until they are light brown.

Once the ornaments have dried, have the children remove any grease with a small piece of clear cellophane tape. Markers or paint can be applied to the top and sides once the ornaments have dried. Finally, attach a magnet to the backs. You can use the ornaments themselves to help measure the size of the piece of magnetic tape necessary; magnetic tape is attached by peeling off the backing. Magnetic tape can be purchased very inexpensively in most hardware departments or hardware stores. With small magnets, simply select one that will fit on the back and attach it with white glue.

◉ Felt and Fabric Ornamental Magnets

Felt and fabric ornamental magnets make especially attractive flowers, leaves, and suns as well as wreaths, menorahs, candles, valentines, and other holiday gifts. The children may want to help collect fabric and felt scraps to match card themes.

Materials

> Small scraps of felt and/or lightweight fabric
>
> Scissors that will cut felt and fabric easily
>
> Decorations such as movable eyes, sequins, ribbons, and yarn
>
> Heavyweight paper or lightweight tag board
>
> Optional: nontoxic fabric glue

Procedures

Encourage the children to plan how they will use the felt and fabric to make a small ornament. They may want to draw sketches of their ornaments. Have children cut out a piece of heavyweight paper or lightweight tag board to serve as the backing. The backing should be no larger than one-and-one-half inches in diameter.

Once children have cut out the paper or tag board backing, they should use it as a pattern for cutting out the felt or fabric background. Fasten the background to the backing with fabric glue. Next, decorate the fabric or felt with permanent markers or other decorations before joining some magnetic tape or a small magnet to the backing.

◎ Plastic Ornamental Magnets

Plastic ornamental magnets are very easy to make out of flexible plastic lids. Young children may need assistance cutting the plastic, but even three- or four-year-olds can decorate it.

Materials

> Flexible, clean, and opaque plastic lids (like those found on many round oatmeal, frosting, and stuffing mix containers)
>
> Scissors strong enough to cut the plastic
>
> Fine-tipped permanent markers

Procedures

Have children design their cards and figure out where the plastic ornamental magnets will be placed. These ornaments can be a little larger than those made out of baker's clay, felt, or fabric because the plastic is quite light. Magnetic tape and small magnets can support plastic ornaments up to two inches in diameter.

Encourage children to make construction paper drafts of their cards and plastic magnets. Then provide the children with markers, lids, and scissors. They should trace the construction paper model on the plastic and cut out the plastic base. As children decorate the plastic, you will quickly discover how easily the ink can smear. I always have students who end up with more of the ink on their fingers than on the plastic. Finally, let the children attach some magnetic tape or a small magnet and double-sided tape to the back of the plastic.

◎ Papier-Mâché Magnets

Papier-mâché magnets lend themselves to opaque ornaments or decorations, especially flowers, butterflies, leaves, valentines, or other objects that do not need fine details.

Materials

Heavy tag board or lightweight cardboard food boxes (such as those packaged to hold cereal, cake mix, gelatin, or pudding)

Colored sheets of tissue paper

White glue

Scissors strong enough to cut lightweight cardboard

Optional: liquid starch

Procedures

Have children plan how the magnet will be integrated into the overall design of the card, preferably by making a draft. For the draft, use a white- or ivory-colored sheet of construction paper backing.

The papier-mâché ornaments can be up to one-and-one-quarter inches in diameter, but the children should be cautioned not to make the ornaments thicker than one-eighth inch.

Have children use the construction paper model to trace the base pattern of the ornament on a piece of lightweight cardboard. After cutting out the cardboard, they should dip small pieces of colored tissue paper into liquid starch or a mixture of equal parts of glue and water. Other pieces of tissue paper can be placed on the backing or on more tissue. This process is repeated until the backing is covered. Children enjoy discovering what colors work well together. Children can use pastel-colored tissue to make papier-mâché magnets that resemble rice paper.

Decorative Pins

A small baker's clay, felt, fabric, plastic, or papier-mâché gift fastened to a small safety pin can grace lapels or hats. Decorative pins can be made for many different occasions. Some children have included a message urging the recipient to think of or remember something when they wear the pin: "Whenever you wear this pin, think about how much I love you." Some children like to think of decorative pins as award pins and may want to write a certificate or an award with the card. They may want to look at other certificates and awards for models. As with other projects, the children need to decide how the decorative pin can be integrated into the design of the card and how the message and the pin can complement one another.

The same basic techniques and materials for creating ornamental magnets are useful here, with some minor differences. Decorative pins are often worn on blouses, dresses, or lapels, and on caps, hats, jackets, and ties. You may want to point out to children that only very small, lightweight pins are worn on ties.

Decorative pins generally need to be smaller than ornamental magnets. A single safety pin can only hold a small amount. Children should also not color the safety pin with a magic marker. One child who did created a permanent decoration on her mother's blouse when the ink rubbed off of the pin. Finally, only new safety pins should be used.

◉ Baker's Clay Pins and Felt/Fabric Ornamental Pins

For baker's clay pins, the base rod of the pin should be inserted into the back of the baker's clay ornament prior to baking. If necessary, the ornament can be baked face down. When the ornament has dried, add a piece of masking tape for reinforcement between the open rod of the safety pin and the baker's clay.

There are two different ways that a safety pin can be attached to a felt or fabric ornamental pin; you can sew one metal base rod of the safety pin directly to the cloth or join them with a very strong piece of masking tape or a piece of cloth tape.

◉ Plastic Pins

Transparent or masking tape is suitable for attaching one part of the safety pin to the back of the plastic ornament.

◉ Papier-Mâché Pins

After children have let their papier-mâché ornaments dry, a safety pin will bind with masking tape or transparent tape.

 **Flower Baskets**

This type of greeting card was originally shared by a teacher who taught in rural Yupik Eskimo villages in southwestern Alaska. The one-dimensional paper flower basket holds several flowers, and each stem has a message. The recipient "picks the flowers" placed in the basket to read the messages. Some children also like to write a greeting on the handle of the basket. One variation has a chore written on each stem, such as "I will clean my room." When the recipient wants a chore done, he or she picks a flower and presents it to the gift giver. This activity does not require much original writing and is especially well suited to beginning writers.

Materials

Lightweight cardstock for younger students

Heavier cardstock for older students

Scissors

Crayons, markers, and colored pencils

Procedures

Draw a large oval and then cut out the oval to make the body of the basket. Draw a half-circle about one-half inch in from the edge of the basket (oval) and cut it out to create the handle. You are left with a one-dimensional basket.

The children can make the flowers with scrap paper from the baskets, writing a message on each stem. Long messages can extend from one side of the stem to the other. Children adore writing in tiny print so that the whole message will fit on the stem! You may want the children to write on the stems before they cut them out. The paper often tears when young children try to write on stems that have already been cut out.

I prefer to have children draw the basket freehand rather than use a pattern as this helps them to develop problem-solving skills; this project is slightly more difficult than the doorknob notes. The first couple of times that young children try to make the baskets they are likely to cut off the basket handle.

Two horizontal slits are made in the body of the basket for each flower, which is then woven into the basket. The basket can be given directly to the recipient or hung on a hook or doorknob.

◎ Appreciation Day Cards

Children can either write down chores they will do or messages of love on the stems of the flowers. A poem with each line numbered and written on the flower stems is a nice touch.

◎ May Day Cards

Children can write down things they like about a special person and then deliver or send their baskets so that the baskets arrive on the first day of May.

◎ Valentine's Day Cards

Instead of making flowers to go into the basket, consider having little valentines on the ends of stems with messages similar to those found on hard valentine candies.

◎ Get-Well Cards

For get-well flower baskets, children can write hopes for recovery on each stem. They might say, "I hope you can run around the block soon," or "You'll be back in school in a week."

 **Activity Gift Cards**

Many children enjoy paper-and-pencil activities such as crossword puzzles, finding hidden pictures or words, mazes, and dot-to-dot pictures. Most also enjoy creating activity sheets resembling worksheets. Cards designed specifically for children can successfully include an activity sheet.

Activity cards are appropriate for all occasions when children might give cards to one another. They are good birthday cards, especially for younger friends or siblings.

Materials

Paper

Crayons and markers

Sample activity sheets (crossword puzzles, hidden pictures, hidden words, mazes, and dot-to-dot pictures)

Optional: rulers or straight edges

Procedures

Have children plan the overall theme of the card. For example, if a child wants to make a May Day card, he or she might create a card with a floral scene. Children then need to figure out what kind of activity sheet to include. For Halloween, they may wish to make to make a hidden picture activity sheet to find pumpkins. Children may want to look at sample activity sheets before they create their own.

It is necessary for children to decide if they will attach the activity sheet to the card or simply lay it in the center of the card. Have students draft the card and activity sheet.

Get-Well Cards

Activity cards give the recipient something fun to do and a reminder of the love and care that went into making the activity sheets. They are a very nice gift for a child who is housebound due to illness.

 Bon Voyage Cards

Activity cards can also be a great bon voyage gift for a child moving away. In one class, children actually did research about the location where their classmate was moving to and put together activity sheets about the destination. In this case, the kids turned a writing activity into a social studies project.

 **African Proverb Necklaces**

African proverb necklaces consist of several proverbs written on pieces of heavy paper or tag board joined to a leather thong or heavy string. The recipient then cuts apart the proverbs from the card and attaches them to make a necklace. This is a good project for a unit on African culture. According to legend, wearing a proverb necklace will grant you good fortune.

 Materials

> Heavy construction paper, poster board, or tag board (empty cereal boxes work well)
>
> Scissors
>
> Markers and crayons
>
> Twine, leather thongs, or yarn
>
> Commercially produced books of proverbs
>
> Student-produced books of proverbs
>
> Optional: beads

◉ Procedures

Have children collect and write proverbs that they feel would be appropriate for the intended recipients. Children may want to spend several weeks collecting and possibly even writing their own proverbs. It is fun to create a class book of proverbs that children can refer to for this and other projects.

Children should plan the design of the card. They also need to think about whether or not they are going to put the proverbs sheet on the cover or message portion of the card or as a freestanding insert.

Next, children should select six to eight proverbs that they feel would be appropriate for the recipient. They might want to select proverbs that match the occasion for the card or the personality of the recipient. I find that some children prefer to give very serious proverbs while other youngsters prefer humorous or even whimsical sayings.

Have the children write a message and design a card. They will need to leave enough space to write instructions on how to assemble the proverb necklace. As part of the card, they should select or write the proverbs for the necklace and then prepare the proverb necklace.

Make the necklace by cutting out a piece of cardstock or heavy tag board that is the same size as the card. The piece of cardstock should be at least six inches high and five inches wide. Have children divide the cardstock into strips, each at least one-and-one-half inches high and two-and-one-half inches long. Children may want to make individual background designs on each proverb strip. Next, write the proverbs on the strips (Figure 10–3). A hole is then punched into each strip, and a string attached to the card. Children need to measure the string to make sure it is the right length. Beads can be attached to the string if the beads are included with the card.

The final step is for the children to write instructions for the proverb necklace assembly somewhere on the card. They can even draw a picture showing how to put together the necklace.

An apple a day
keeps the doctor away.

Starye a cold.
Feed a fever.

Time is money.

Distance makes the
heart grow tender.

You can catch more
flies with honey than
with vinegar.

Be kind to
your neighbors

Cover your head
when you go outside.

Sticks and stones
will break my bones
but words will never
hurt me.

Time flies when
you're having fun.

Be young at
heart.

It's never too
late to learn.

Don't put off until
tomorrow what you
can do today.

Figure 10-3

 **Fan Cards**

Fan cards are both fans and cards, and they are very simple to make. There is a fan on one side and a message on the other. This type of card was originally designed by a teacher working with young children in Mexico City. They are especially appropriate in warm weather.

Materials

Construction paper or lightweight cardstock

Markers

White school glue

Popsicle sticks

Large doilies

Paper for making decorations on the fan portion of the card

Ribbons

Gold seals

Writing paper

Procedures

Have children think about who the recipient of the fan will be and whether or not that person would use a fan. For example, a relative who is always complaining about the heat would probably love a fan card. Have the children fold the doilies to look like a fan (they may want to look at a fan). Popsicle sticks are glued on to make the edges of the fan, and ribbons and seals make good adornments. Encourage the children as they are making the fans to think about the accompanying poem or letter they will write. Once the fan has been finished, the children should draft their message and, when satisfied with the draft, write a final message on a sheet of writing paper attached to the back of the fan.

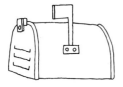

References

Arendt, Helene and Mary McCarthy. 1995. *Between Friends: Correspondence of Hannah Arendt and Mary McCarthy 1949–1975.* New York: Harcourt Brace.

Atwell, Nancie. 1987. *In the Middle.* Portsmouth, NH: Boynton/Cook.

De Beauvoir, Simone, ed. *Witness to My Life: The Letters of Jean-Paul Sartre to Simone de Beauvoir.* Translated by Lee Fahnestock and Norman McAfee. New York: Macmillan.

Dixon, C., and D. Nessel. 1983. *Language Experience Approach to Reading and Writing: LEA for ESL.* Hayward, CA: Alemany Press.

Graves, Donald H. 1994. *A Fresh Look at Writing.* Portsmouth, NH: Heinemann.

———. 1983. *Writing: Teachers and Children at Work.* Portsmouth, NH: Heinemann.

Hannf, Helene. 1970. *84 Charing Cross Road.* New York: Penguin.

Hassler, John. 1985. *A Green Journey.* New York: Ballentine.

Hewitt, Geof. 1994. *A Portfolio Primer: Teaching, Collecting, and Assessing Student Writing.* Portsmouth, NH: Heinemann.

Hubbard, Ruth Shagoury, and Karen Ernst, eds. 1996. *New Entries: Learning by Writing and Drawing.* Portsmouth, NH: Heinemann.

Hudelson, S. 1989. *Write On: Children Writing in ESL.* Englewood Cliffs, NJ: Center for Applied Linguistics and Prentice Hall Regents.

Johnson, Paul. 1993. *Literacy Through the Book Arts.* Portsmouth, NH: Heinemann.

Nakazawa, Keiko. 1995. *Best Greeting Cards: Pop Up.* Tokyo, Japan: Ondorisha Publishers Ltd.

Plath, Sylvia. 1992. *Letters Home: Correspondence 1950–1963.* New York: HarperCollins.

Rigg, Patricia, ed. 1989. *When They Don't All Speak English.* Urbana, IL: National Council of Teachers of English.

Smallwood, Betty. 1991. *The Literature Collection: A Read-Aloud Guide for Multicultural Classrooms.* Reading, MA: Addison Wesley Longman.

Smith, Frank. 1978. *Writing and the Writer.* New York: Holt, Rinehart, and Winston.

Van Allen, R., and C. Allen. 1976. *Language Experience Activities.* Boston: Houghton Mifflin.